MW00891684

"You don't know what a blessing this has been. It has been such a message of confirmation and of comfort! Earlier this year, my Dad told me to continue being busy for God. Don't worry about timetables and how things look with regards to not being sent a mate…. Isn't it awesome to realize that God is more than enough for you? I just loved your words and I could write on and on…just wanted you to know that your testimony has blessed me and so many others!"

"Thank you for this testimony. I am single now after separation from my husband. Reading your story is very comforting to me."

"Thank you for that encouraging word. I'm a turning-27-single myself and I could identify with all the struggles you went through. Most of my friends can also relate to your valley experiences as a single. Praise God for the love and assurance of His presence every day. Although loneliness is a physical reality, when a woman chooses to run to the even more real presence of God by faith, she'll learn to embrace the joys and challenges of single-blessedness. I realize I am only beginning this journey of discovering these, and I thank God that he's my guide and fellow sojourner. I hope you'll continue to minister to singles and point them to Jesus!"

"I just read *The Blessings of Loneliness*, and I appreciate your sharing such profound words of wisdom. I have been in the season of singleness for what seems like an eternity. While seeking God to satisfy the desire for a mate, I too discovered His love for me, and now I can't stop talking about Him. God bless you in your endeavors."

THE BLESSINGS
OF LONELINESS

THE BLESSINGS OF LONELINESS

REACHING WITHIN THE PAIN TO FIND CONTENTMENT IN CHRIST

SABRINA MCDONALD

CHISELBOOKS

CHISELBOOKS is a privately owned publishing company:

The author of this publication is responsible for all editing and proofreading and responsible for any errors in the finished product.

Unless otherwise stated, scripture references are taken from the New American Standard Bible, © 1960, 1962, 1963, 1968, 1971, 1972, 1973, 1975, 1977, 1995, by the Lockman foundation. Used by permission. (www.Lockman.org)

Details in some anecdotes and stories have been changed to protect the identities of the persons involved.

Printed in the United States of America.

ISBN 978-1-5010-2334-7

To my late husband, David Beasley.
You were my biggest cheerleader and supported me through all the blood, sweat, and tears. This book could not have been written without your grace-filled love and encouragement.

And to my new love, Robbie McDonald.
I'm so thankful to have you in my life. Your love and support gives me strength. You have been a blessing to me since the first day we met. I can't wait to see what God does through our story.

Table of Contents

Chapter 1

Blessings in Disguise

"If anyone wishes to come after Me,
he must deny himself, and take up his cross and follow Me."
-Matthew 16:24

Loneliness is not a blessing … at least not the kind of blessing that brings great happiness in and of itself. I must put it bluntly because as I have attempted to publish this book, I've found that the title is deceiving, often being misconceived to be a series of suggestions on how to give up on marriage and pursue singleness for life, but being a married woman myself, that is not at all the intention of this book.

Loneliness is a personal wilderness that takes pain and suffering to endure. It can crush your heart and mind under its heaviness if you try to handle it in human terms alone. Loneliness is hard. C.S. Lewis often used isolation and loneliness as a description of what he thought Hell would be like. Yet all of us must go through it at some point—married and single alike. It is no respecter of persons.

But within the wilderness of this journey, there are miracles that take place—manna from heaven, water from rocks, pillars of fire. These are the privileged times that sufferers have the honor of seeing God work on their behalf, the honor of being rescued by Him. These are the blessings that my title refers to. To put it another way, they are the jewels that you find deep in the dark cold mines of life. You won't find treasure unless you're willing to get dirty and endure pain.

I had my first real experience with loneliness in my early twenties. I had six roommates in two years—each one making her exit from my domicile by way of the church altar. I felt like I was living in a boarding house for engaged women. I donned a bridesmaid gown in at least a dozen weddings, often standing as maid of honor—doting, counseling, and planning for the bride. As a singer, I was in dozens.

I remember the first time a girl moved in with me who wasn't engaged. She didn't even have a serious boyfriend. I thought I had finally found a roommate who might stay for a while, but a few months into our living arrangements she met the man she would marry only a year later. I laughed because I wondered if girls were moving in with me because they thought I might bring them good luck! Although my house was always full, I felt very much alone.

Eventually, though, it was my turn for matrimony. I met the man who would be my best friend, lover, and father of my two children. We had a wonderful marriage filled with contented joy and unusually blessed happiness. We thanked God for each other every day and wondered why He would so richly bless us when others struggled.

For eight years we enjoyed each other, and then one day with my two-year-old son and three-month-old baby girl in my arms, the police visited my home delivering the news that my husband was killed instantly in a head-on collision as he made his way back to the city from a work appointment. The love of my life was dead.

The rooms at my house were full many days after that, but there was a black hole in my heart that could not be filled with friends or church members. After all those many lonely single years, God finally gifted me with the perfect fit, only to have him taken from me prematurely. In my mind, I debated the old saying, "It is better to have loved and lost than never to have loved at all." I wasn't sure this kind of loss was worth it. The love was inebriating, but the loneliness sobering. One made the other so much worse, but the memories, the experiences—all the gains, I wouldn't give them up if I had to do it over again.

I lived as a widow and single mom of two preschoolers for three years until God brought another widower in my path, Robbie McDonald. In less than a year we were married and blended our two families. In many ways Robbie filled the void of single living, but stepfamily living can actually bring out other forms of loneliness, like feeling left out or misunderstood.

Loneliness is painful. God didn't create people to be unaccompanied. He said Himself in Genesis 2:23 after He formed Adam from the earth, "It is not good for man to be alone." So, to remedy the problem, God created a helper for him—Eve, who was custom made for the one who would call her "bone of my bone and flesh of my flesh." It's natural to desire that kind of closeness with a man—as if you were filled with his very bones and covered with his flesh.

There were times when I fell on my knees and begged God through tears to take my pain away. But God continually used that pain to bring me to the sweetest love affair of my life, not by bringing me a man to fall in love with, but by making me more like the Man who already loved me.

Loneliness is a reminder of the cross, the sacrifice of our own desires for those of the Lord. God can use it to refine our lives, just as fire purifies gold (Malachi 3:3). Jesus tells us in Matthew 16:24-25, "If anyone wishes to come after Me, he must deny himself, and take up his cross and follow Me. For whoever wishes to save his life will lose it; but whoever loses his life for My sake will find it."

Feeling the pain of isolation is a reminder to let go of our own desires and embrace the humility of Christ—a life to be lived as a servant (Philippians 2:7), doing the calling of God with a grateful heart. The fact is, you are single. A spouse has not yet been provided, and until that day comes, if it comes, there is purpose in the life you are living now. That's not to say that marriage should no longer be a desire, but that you should live with an attitude of contentment, embracing all that God has for you to accomplish and receive during this wilderness in life, however long it may last.

So many Christians forget that God calls us to the low places. He calls us to be lowly (Psalm 38:6), to be humble (James 4:6), to be meek (Matthew 4:5 KJV). He even calls us to die (Romans 6:3-5). None of these come easily, and they almost always require pain. But in return we've been promised recognition, grace, inheritance, and everlasting life. 1 Peter 5:5-6 tells us that God will give grace to the humble and in due time, He will lift them up.

The Christian music group Caedmon's Call recorded a song called "Valleys Fill First," reminding us when rain falls, the water flows to the lowest places first. Those in the valley will be the first to receive the refreshing waters washing over them. The blood of Christ was meant to flow to those who are hurting and struggling. Jesus said, "It is not those who are well who need a physician, but those who are sick" (Luke 5:31). The only way to experience healing is to first experience infirmity.

I am one who has felt His healing touch in my life. Even though I have experienced times of unexplainable loneliness in an earthly sense, the void was more than filled, even overflowing, with satisfaction and a sense of belonging in Christ. Twice now I have had to make this journey through the darkest fears and hurts that could plague my life, and God has clearly shown me through various circumstances that my destiny is no accident. The miracle is that my satisfaction and fulfillment comes within the pain, not without it.

At my first husband's funeral, I requested a song that had been on my heart even before his passing. The words repeat over and over "He who began a good in work in you will be faithful to complete it" (a paraphrase of Philippians 1:6). As the words were sung, I lifted up my hands to the Lord. Many onlookers mistook my reaction as some kind of super strong faith-filled act of praise and worship, but what I was really doing was surrendering—I was throwing my hands out to say, "I have nothing, and all I can do is surrender to you. There is nothing else to cling to, and I'm praying that what your word has promised in the words of this song is true."

The Apostle Paul was a man of God who personally understood the pain and value of suffering. He wrote about the power of weakness in 2 Corinthians 12:7-10:

> *For this reason, to keep me from exalting myself, there was given me a thorn in the flesh, a messenger of Satan to torment me—to keep me from exalting myself! Concerning this I implored the Lord three times that it might leave me. And He has said to me, "My grace is sufficient for you, for power is perfected in weakness." Most gladly, therefore, I will rather boast about my weaknesses, so that the power of Christ may dwell in me. Therefore I am well content with weaknesses, with insults, with distresses, with persecutions, with difficulties, for Christ's sake; for when I am weak, then I am strong.*

Like the Apostle Paul's personal affliction, loneliness can be the conduit through which God shows His greatest power in your life. Perhaps you have also asked God numerous times to send you a spouse so that

4

your pain might leave you. I know I did. But perhaps God is giving the same response that he gave Paul, employing you to find purpose in the pain of suffering alone—not that singleness will last an entire lifetime, but to bask in all that it has to offer the spirit and soul right now until the day comes that the Lord releases you.

Through the next 11 chapters, I am going to share with you the lessons that others and I have learned during our experiences with loneliness. My own personal pain forced me to see areas in my life that needed change, and the loneliness drove me to find a deeper love and acceptance in Christ than I have ever known.

In this book, I hope to explain how blessings can come *through* the pain of loneliness and rejection. It is not a book on how to resolve your longings and cure your sadness or even numb it by giving up on the idea of marriage altogether. The reason is because in order to experience the blessings, you must be willing to shoulder the pain. It is not by avoiding the battles that we gain ground, but by fighting, inching forward with every thrust of the sword. I can testify from my own experience and by the testimony and authority of the Scripture that if you will embrace what is explained in this book, you, too, will experience the blessings of loneliness

Chapter 2

The Blessings of Brokenness

"The sacrifices of God are a broken spirit, a broken and contrite heart—
These, O God, You will not despise."
-Psalm 51:17

Chonda was like most American young women. She grew up believing that she would get married and have children like the other women in her family. She went through college and graduate school and started a successful career. When Chonda started attending the singles group at her new church, she was already in her mid-twenties and still not married. As she looked around at her friends, she worried, seeing that most of them had already started families.

Chonda had always considered herself independent and felt pride in her quirky personal style, but for the first time in her life, she began to wonder, *"Maybe there's something wrong with me. Maybe that's why no one wants to marry me."*

Being a new girl at the singles group, Chonda was asked on plenty of dates, and she saw each one as an opportunity to secure a man to marry. With each serious relationship, she allowed her new insecurities to morph her into whatever her suitor wanted. When she dated a hard-rocker, Chonda listened to heavy metal music. When she dated a lawyer, she gave up the heavy metal and listened to classical. She even started wearing glasses, even though the lenses had no prescriptions, only clear glass. When Chonda dated a body-builder, she cut her hair and became obsessed with her physique.

Finally, after dozens of failed relationships, Chonda looked at herself in the mirror and asked, "Who am I? What have I become?" This once carefree woman was now struggling with an identity crisis.

It was Chonda's desire to control her destiny that drove her to seek the approval of her suitors. She viewed her singleness as a reflection of her self-worth, and so she did everything she could to find a way through male companionship to complete what she thought was broken. The problem, however, was that she forgot to whom her destiny belonged—the Lord Jesus. Even though she was a Christian, Chonda took her future into her own hands and experienced painful consequences—all to satisfy her own desires on *her* schedule, not God's.

I remember being bound in the same trap with an ex-boyfriend. Although we only dated for six months, I was painfully jealous and worked tirelessly to win him back for two years. As I watched him interact with various other women, I constantly mourned the fact that he rejected me. In my mind his refusal meant there was something wrong with me, and I thought by winning him back, I could prove that I was good enough to be wanted.

Thoughts bombarded my mind regarding how I could meet his standards so that he would date me again—how I could be more attractive and likeable. I believed if I worked hard enough, I could control the situation and prove to him that I was what he wanted, but no matter what I did, nothing was good enough for him. There was always something I could do better, add, or take away… the list of improvements was endless.

I looked around at other women in the church. They appeared to be superior in every way. It seemed as if all the ladies had themselves together, but I was a wreck. As I compared myself, I always came up lacking. One girl had a brighter smile; one was more stylish; one was trimmer; one was friendlier; one was funnier.

The challenge to be the perfect woman consumed my mind. Even my relationship with God became a way to market myself. Instead of growing spiritually because I loved Christ, I was hoping to become godlier so that I could add that to my relationship resume, applying the principles of God's word to impress a man.

My pride made me believe that if I could just become better than all of the other women, I could have any man I wanted. I could even win back my ex-boyfriend and finally prove to him that I was worth a second chance. Even though I knew in my heart that a relationship with him was not what God wanted for my life, I would not accept his rejection of me. At the time, I thought giving up would be a sign of agreement that I wasn't good enough. In my mind, an attitude of acceptance would mean that I had lost the battle and agreed to defeat ... and my pride wasn't going to allow that.

I tried every improvement to succeed in getting him back, and nothing worked. I felt completely helpless. Once I asked him, "What's wrong with me? I have overcome every criticism you ever had. I've become the woman of your dreams. Why don't you want to be with me?"

He responded, "It's true. You've become everything I ever wanted. You've overcome your weaknesses and grown to be a great woman of God. Honestly, I've considered getting back together with you many times. I even prayed, asking God if this is the right thing for me. But no matter how many times I pray, I don't feel a peace about it. God just won't let me be with you."

That statement scared me. You see, for all the work I was doing to improve, I wasn't seeking *God's* will for my life; I was seeking my own. Why was I trying to force marriage with someone that God didn't want me to be with? Was I so desperate to save my pride that I was willing to seek something beyond God's perfect will? I knew that was not what I wanted for my life. The Holy Spirit stirred within me, and conviction finally grabbed hold of my heart.

I wasted two years of working just so I could win back a man that God didn't want me to be with. The time I spent focusing on my pride, my desires, and myself could have been used to seek God's will, instead of fighting it. The Father cannot and will not be controlled by *our* actions and wants, so why do we spend our time resisting Him? If I had only sought God's desires first, I could have used that valuable time to glorify Him, instead of my personal agenda. In that I would have found peace and purpose, but instead I only found frustration. And for what purpose? To avoid loneliness, which could have provided a much richer harvest had I valued the time I had to do the work of the Lord.

The conversation I had with my ex-boyfriend brought me to the end of myself. I felt like I had used everything in my power to climb the tallest mountain in my life only to take one final step over the precipice of death, falling into the valley. I hit the bottom. It was impossible to go on. I had used up all of my resources, my strength, and my breath—I had nothing left. It was as if my arms and legs were broken...

… and that's exactly where I needed to be.

The Battle with Pride

Perhaps you can identify with Chonda and me. If you're experiencing loneliness, then more than likely, you have felt a great deal of rejection. Perhaps you've allowed comparisons with other girls to depress you or make you feel inadequate. You may have even been angry with God, making way for bitterness to settle into your relationship with Him. In either case, your battle isn't with loneliness or with God. You're battle is with yourself. Pride has made you believe that *you* have the power to control your own destiny.

Many people understand pride to mean that you think of yourself as better than others, like walking around with your nose in the air. That's not completely wrong—haughtiness is a part of pride. But it's much broader than that.

Pride most often occurs when a person puts herself in the center of her universe, around which everything else revolves. She starts to think she knows what her needs are better than God, and seek her own will, instead of His.

Perhaps you and I don't consciously think thoughts like these, but they exist in the heart. For example, Chonda basically felt like God was lacking in His job, so she took control. She was determined to find a husband no matter who she had to become to get one. She abandoned God's calling because she was afraid that His plans might include loneliness. Eventually she suffered greatly for turning from her true purpose.

I also allowed pride to take over as I exalted my own needs to such a lofty position that fulfilling those needs became the greatest passion of my life. I had fallen into the "I deserve" mindset. I saw what others had— namely male companionship and attention—and I wanted it for myself. Instead of being grateful for the gift of singleness that I had been given, at some point I decided that God's gift wasn't what I wanted, and as a result, I, too, suffered great hurt.

The cure for pride is brokenness, which brings about humility. Proverbs 11:2 says, "When pride comes, then comes dishonor, but with the humble is wisdom." In her book, *Brokenness: The Heart God Revives*, Nancy Leigh DeMoss describes brokenness in terms of taming a horse:

When we speak of a stallion being 'broken,' we don't mean that someone physically breaks its legs; we mean that the horse's will has been broken—that it is now compliant and submissive to the wishes of its rider. In the same sense, true brokenness is the breaking of my self-will, so that the life and spirit of the Lord Jesus may be released through me. It is my humble and obedient response to the conviction of God's Word and His Holy Spirit.

Chonda and I were so determined to be in a relationship that we were willing to change anything, morph into whatever our suitors wanted. But that is not what God wants for His children. Married or unmarried, God gave each of us a certain personality with specific gifts and callings. We were made to glorify Him, and He molds us to reflect *His* glory (Romans 9:20-21) and to accomplish *His* will, not our own. When we give up those inherent characteristics, then we cannot be used by God as He has called us to be used. Marriage on those terms is not worth the price. No man could ever fulfill the longings in your heart compared to the fulfillment of God's purposes.

Christ Living in Us

It took coming to the end of myself to teach this over-achieving, aggressive, prideful woman that I needed to find fulfillment in Christ, not in my abilities to capture the attention of a man. I was so tired of working, so tired of being less than adequate. There was nothing left for me to do but to give up and admit that I wasn't able to reach my goal, but that's exactly what I needed to do. When *I* stopped working, that's when *Christ* would work through me.

In John 15:5 Jesus says, "For apart from me you can do nothing." I am a sinful creature, and the only good I have in me is the Spirit that lives within me. As Romans 3:12 says, "All have turned aside, together they have become useless; there is none who does good, there is not even one." Because the flesh is fallible, it is impossible to achieve true peace, no matter how much work is involved. There is simply not enough power in the flesh to remain in control, and that's when we are forced to submit to the Spirit.

It was such sweet peace the day I surrendered my search for a spouse to the Lord. I simply confessed out loud, "I'm finished! I can't do this anymore. I'm not perfect, and I'm never going to be perfect. Lord, I don't have what it takes to find a mate; I give up." I finally realized I had nothing to offer anyone—the only thing I had worth giving was Christ who lived in me.

The most beautiful part was that by surrendering, I no longer had to worry about failing—Christ had already made up for all my shortcomings. I no longer had to worry about trying to accomplish perfection in order to win someone over—Christ was whole and complete and didn't need my work. I finally realized that a relationship with Him is all that I need, and that was something I already had and couldn't be taken away from me.

The way I was behaving toward Christ during that time reminds me of a very ill person who refuses to go to the doctor. She tries to convince herself that she isn't sick. When that is no longer deniable, she tries to convince herself that she can take care of it and heal herself. When the pain gets too great, she finally breaks down and calls the doctor who lives next door, and he is able to give her all that she needs to be well. Why had I waited so long to seek the Doctor who could heal all of my hurts? The healing I was experiencing had only just begun.

True Healing

God loves the brokenhearted. Psalm 51:17 says, "The sacrifices of God are a broken spirit, a broken and contrite heart—These, O God, You will not despise." The intimacy with Christ while undergoing His healing is an unspeakably beautiful encounter. Every ounce of pain and rejection I felt was worth the nurture of my sweet Jesus. When I had fallen and was crushed and hurting, the Shepherd came to rescue me. It was in those times when I stopped talking and listened to His words of comfort. I stopped rushing through life and took the time to find shelter under His great arms.

I love the depictions of shepherds carrying sheep on their shoulders because that's exactly how I felt, as if I was being carried by Christ Himself. I was no longer in control of where I was going—He was. I was completely limp, yet finally making progress in the will of God. I felt so close to Him that if I closed my eyes, sometimes I could almost feel His breath against my face. Although I knew Christ was the one who allowed my brokenness, it was worth the hurt to experience His loving care and miraculous healing.

Those early years of rejection before my first marriage were just a small preparation for the depth of loneliness that was to come. Psalm 34:18-19 says, "The Lord is near to the brokenhearted and saves those who are crushed in spirit. Many are the afflictions of the righteous, but the Lord delivers him out of them all." When a spouse dies, the loneliness is crushing. I don't know how people survive it without Jesus in their lives because the hope of Christ was the only thing that kept me from going out of my mind. The Lord walked with me every single step of the way, and spoke to me with tenderness and compassion and listened to my anger and questions with patience.

Even though God allows us to experience such pain, He isn't hard-hearted toward our hurt—He feels our aches and cries for us, just like He did for his friend Lazarus. In John 11, Martha and Mary sent a message to Jesus saying that their brother Lazarus (whom the Bible says Jesus loved) was sick. Jesus responded, "This sickness is not to end in death, but for the glory of God so that the Son of God may be glorified by it." Not long after that, Lazarus died.

When Jesus did finally come, Mary and Martha were grieved. They both said, "Lord, if you had been here, my brother would not have died" (vs. 21 and 32). As Jesus saw the grieving that took place, He was deeply moved and He wept (v. 35, 38).

Jesus wasn't weeping for a dead Lazarus. Lazarus was a man of God, so there was no doubt of his eternal destiny. Not only that, but Jesus knew that He was about to raise Lazarus from the dead. Only moments later, He Himself called Lazarus from the grave and restored life to him. So why did He cry? I believe Jesus was weeping with compassion, not only for Mary and Martha, but for every single person who has ever had to experience the loss that death brings. He was hurting for a world that has been riddled with death. Mary, Martha, and the others were hurting and grieving, and Jesus' heart ached for them. After Lazarus' resurrection, many Jews came to believe in Jesus as the Son of God. Jesus didn't have to allow Lazarus to die. He could have healed him, but this pain was necessary so that His power would be glorified.

Don't you think Lazarus was thankful for his healing even if Jesus allowed him to die? And he was most likely glad to be a tool so that others may come to know Christ. That's the question we must ask yourself—are you pleased with your loneliness if it is necessary to glorify God and bring His message to those whom you influence?

I saw a powerful impact in many lives after the tragic death of my husband. Several friends were challenged by the advice in one of his letters that was published after his death. Many who saw the kind of relationship we had felt conviction to have better marriages and let go of petty disagreements. Pastors and counselors asked to share his advice in weddings and counseling sessions. I've had numerous opportunities to share God's principles for spiritual growth and healthy marriages, and I continue to minister to other widows who are feeling the depths of grief.

I did not enjoy being widowed any more than I enjoyed singleness the first time, In fact, it was much worse. But if just one person comes to know Christ as Savior and Lord because of that terrible tragedy, it was worth all the tears and brokenheartedness that this one person had to endure.

Brokenness is Necessary

Brokenness is the first necessary step to accepting the blessings of loneliness. It's what gives you the ability to receive and understand all of the other blessings. Unfortunately, most Christians aren't willing to come to this beautiful state, but unless we are broken people, God cannot use us. For those who continue to try to shoulder loneliness without brokenness, they will find it a heavy burden that is immobilizing. Only the broken will have the burden lifted and be carried by the Caregiver.

Several years ago, I learned how to make pottery. It amazed me to witness a usable, beautiful vase come from a ball of clay. At first the clay is hard and uneven, so before you can begin molding, you must soften it by cutting the lumps in half, putting the pieces on top of each other and kneading them together. Over and over again you break the clay and knead it until it is soft and workable.

In Jeremiah 18:3-6, the Lord God says, "Behold, like the clay in the potter's hand, so are you in My hand, O house of Israel." Just as the clay must be kneaded and softened, we also must be broken before we can be used. Without this process, the potter's clay is worth no more than the earth on a trodden pathway. Nothing can be accomplished with it. But once we are softened, the Potter can wield us into whatever shape He needs, whether it be a water pot, cup, platter, or vase. Best of all, we not only accomplish our purpose in life, but we also become a beautiful work of art.

Weightlifters understand brokenness more than anyone. In order to become stronger, the muscle tissue must be ripped (or broken), and when it heals, that wound actually forms a stronger bond than it had before. These tiny rips happen all throughout the muscle tissue, and as a result what you get are stronger, fuller muscles. Day by day, weightlifters purposely break their bodies so that they may grow stronger.

The same is true for our spiritual lives. In order to grow, we must be broken and healed, broken and healed, and when we are healed through Christ, we become more resilient in Him and accustomed (or trained) to do His will. Hebrews 12:5-13 explains the necessity of this kind of discipline:

> "My son, do not regard lightly the discipline of the Lord, nor faint when you are reproved by Him; for those whom the Lord loves He disciplines. And He scourges every son whom He receives." It is for discipline that you endure; God deals with you as with sons; for what son is there whom his father does not discipline? But if you are without discipline, of which all have become partakers, then you are illegitimate children and not sons. Furthermore, we had earthly fathers to discipline us, and we respected them; shall we not much rather be subject to the Father of spirits, and live? For they disciplined us for a short time as seemed best to them, but He disciplines us for our good, so that we may share His holiness. All discipline for the moment seems not to be joyful, but sorrowful; yet to those who have been trained by it, afterwards it yields the peaceful fruit of righteousness. Therefore, strengthen the hands that are weak and the knees that are feeble, and make straight paths for your feet, so that the limb which is lame may not be put out of joint, but rather be healed.

When you feel sadness from loneliness, that emotion urges you to seek love in the only place where you can find it—in Christ. If you do this over and over, you will become trained to find your affection and acceptance in Him alone. And as a result, the fruit of that discipline comes when we begin to understand that we don't need earthly love to fulfill us or to give us peace, but our every need is met in Christ. The more we discipline ourselves to find love in Christ, the more we grow stronger in Him day by day.

In the book *His Intimate Presence*, Bill Bright explains this concept:

14

Jesus said, "I am the vine, and my Father is the gardener. He cuts off every branch that doesn't produce fruit, and He prunes the branches that do bear fruit so they will produce even more' (John 15:1-2). Pruning can be painful and discouraging, but if we want to produce abundant fruit for the Lord, we must undergo discipline. We must withstand trials to pass the test. As all good earthly parents know, loving discipline and the lessons from life are necessary to produce mature children. So it is with God.

How to Receive Brokenness

Brokenness begins with humility. This is a word that literally means "of low degree" or "low estate." When seeking lowliness, the goal is not to be sad and depressed, but instead to see ourselves in light of who Christ is—the way a newborn's fingers look so tiny against her father's hands. When we are in a state of brokenness, it is clear that we are incomparable to God—we can see that He is so much bigger than we are.

Humility opens our eyes to our need for help. When you humble yourself in this way, the Bible promises that He will exalt you, or to put it another way, lift you up. (James 4:10). A person doesn't need a savior if she doesn't need saving. Brokenness helps us recognize the fact that we can't achieve fulfillment of our purpose without the sole direction and guidance of the Holy Spirit. Lowliness changes our perception so we can rightfully see where we belong in our relationship with the Father.

So how does one go about seeking humility? First, you must *accept your pain.* When experiencing heartache, our natural tendency is to put on a happy face, trying to forget or pretend the hurt isn't there. But the best way to alleviate the aching soul is to lean into it. Let the pressure cave in and the tears flow. Psalm 126:5 says, "They that sow in tears shall reap in joy" (KJV).

Don't try to act as if loneliness doesn't sometimes stab you in the heart. Denial of the hurt will only make you bitter and hard. But by confessing your need for a healer for your broken heart, Christ steps in and provides you with His soothing balm. You can't heal yourself, so don't try to. Jesus is there waiting to help you through all the tears. All you need to do is pray and ask Him to minister to you.

Leaning into the pain does not mean that you feel sorry for yourself all of the time. It does mean, however, that you take the feelings of hurt that

15

you have in your heart and allow God to use it in your life to draw you closer to Him. Talk to God. Tell Him how much you ache. Explain how difficult this burden is to carry. But remember to listen to Him, too. The Lord has a message for you as you work through the sorrow—it's a message of comfort and of conviction. There is a reason you are in this battle. There is a purpose, and only God knows what it is, so listen. Seek the answer, and you will find it.

The more time you spend with the Lord, the more you will take your thoughts off of yourself and put them on Him. The weeping draws us to Him, and His presence gives us the joy to sustain our hope. As Psalm 30:5 says, "Weeping may last for the night, but a shout of joy comes in the morning." You see, in Him, we have all that we need, including internal joy and peace, not of earthly circumstances but of simply knowing Christ. When we begin to see the greatness of who He is in light of who we are, then we can't help but worship and praise Him. Allow your agony to point you to Christ, who understands all things (Hebrews 4:15).

In addition, daily consider whether you think about others more than yourself. Loneliness has a way of making a person too self-absorbed, always concerned about his or her own needs, seeking approval and attention from others. Each and every day you must lay down any tendencies to think this way. Then ask the Lord to show you how to love the people in your life and walk in His footsteps, who lowered Himself to accomplish the will of God. (Hebrews 2:9). Ask yourself who you can encourage or serve. Is there someone in your church that could use a word of inspiration? By turning the focus of your life on others, you are putting yourself at the bottom of the priority list, making your life in lower estate than everyone else. Philippians 2:5-8 says:

> *Have this attitude in yourselves which was also in Christ Jesus, who, although He existed in the form of God, did not regard equality with God a thing to be grasped, but emptied himself taking the form of a bond-servant, and being made in the likeness of men. Being found in appearance as a man, He humbled Himself by becoming obedient to the point of death, even death on a cross.*

As you walk the road to brokenness, you will be reminded daily that you are completely dependent on Him. In your dependency, learn to pray throughout the day. 1 Thessalonians 5:17 tells us to "pray without

16

ceasing." That doesn't mean that you should always be kneeling with your eyes closed and head bowed, but it means to be in a continual conversation with the Holy Spirit. This may mean praying in your car, at night while you are lying in bed, in the line at the grocery store—just like talking to a friend who is standing next to you.

You may also want to have a daily time set aside to study God's word, which is the roadmap of life. The Bible is our compass to show the way we should go. By searching God's word for truth and not your own power of reason and critical thinking, you will always be pointed in the right direction. During your times of study, set aside enough time to talk to Jesus without distractions around you. All healthy relationships need time of communication. If you were married, you would have times like these with your spouse, perhaps before bed or in the morning. So you should do the same for the One who loves you more than anyone on this earth could.

In my intimate times with Jesus, I poured out my sorrows. It felt like draining a festering wound. It was messy and ugly—there were tears, red eyes, and bellowing cries—but it felt so good to my infected soul, which had for so long tried to cover the lesions, instead of seeking to find the cure, which is Christ. "He heals the brokenhearted and binds up their wounds" (Psalm 147:3).

I keep a prayer journal which I find keeps my mind on my prayers and thoughts to the Father, instead of wandering in other directions. It also helps me see how God has answered my prayers in the past. However you have to focus your mind during prayer, a healthy relationship with the Father requires honesty and openness on your part.

Another way to grow in brokenness is to learn to glorify the Lord in everything that you do, even the simple tasks. 1 Corinthians 10:31 says, "Whether, then, you eat or drink or whatever you do, do all to the glory of God." Here again is an excellent way to confess out loud the graciousness of God and your need for Him. In the morning, when you wake up, praise God for your life. We so often take for granted that we are alive for another day. Thank him for health, food, children, even the single life. Be grateful for what you do have, instead of complaining about what you lack. It is by God's grace alone that we have anything at all. Let your brokenness yield thanksgiving in your heart no matter what you are doing throughout the day, even the things you may not enjoy. Complainers are usually those who think they deserve more than they have, but a person with a heart of brokenness understand the potential darkness of their own hearts and realize that the good in their lives is undeserved, creating a sense of appreciation for what they do have.

The blessings of brokenness come when we are quiet before the Lord and receive His healing response. The Lord tells us to "be still and know that I am God" (Psalm 46:10 KJV). God talks to us in many different ways, and most of the time it is not through an audible voice. Sometimes hearing His voice comes in the form of just *knowing*, like the previous verse talks about—just by being still we can feel His presence. His healing responses may come in the form of peace that makes everything feel right even though in the world's eyes, it shouldn't. The answers may also come in the form of a thought or sense of feeling. The key is to take time to be with Christ one-on-one to know His voice and to read His word for confirmation.

Let me caution you, however—be aware that during these times there is more than just the responses of God coming to your mind. There are thoughts of the flesh and even temptations that come from Satan. Remember that God will never tell you anything that conflicts with His word. Any message you hear from Him can be verified through the scriptures.

As you seek your purpose in life, Christ will lead you there if you follow Him, whether that is marriage or not. He will never take you to a place that you cannot handle. You have the strength of Christ to sustain you when you are willing to follow His lead. Jesus said, "Come to Me, all who are weary and heavy-laden, and I will give you rest. Take My yoke upon you and learn from Me, for I am gentle and humble in heart, and you will find rest for your souls. For My yoke is easy and My burden is light" (Matthew 11:29).

You will become weary if you try to fit marriage into the plan that you think you deserve in your life. If you're chasing the dream that you created, then you can't very well chase the future that God has for you. Don't miss the great blessings because you are so focused on what you think will make you happy. You must be humble enough to set aside your own wants and desires, even those for marriage and companionship, and be willing to give up anything to follow Him. Only then you will find true contentment in Christ, only then will you experience the blessings of brokenness.

Chapter 3

The Blessings of Suffering

"The Spirit Himself testifies with our spirit that we are children of God, and if children, heirs also, heirs of God and fellow heirs with Christ, if indeed we suffer with Him so that we may also be glorified with Him"
-Romans 8:16-17

Jeremy was counseling Shelly when he fell in love with her. He knew she had emotional problems, but he thought he could help her. They got married with blissful dreams, but only a few months after their glorious honeymoon, Shelly tried to commit suicide. Months of counseling went by, and Shelly got better, but Jeremy was scared. How could he get close to her knowing that she could take herself from him at any moment?

Throughout the next year, Shelly was on suicide watch, and Jeremy learned to put his trust in Christ. Jeremy searched his heart for the Comforter, and learned to depend on the Holy Spirit for his strength. At the end of the year, Jeremy finally felt safe enough again to share his life with his bride, but only days after she was taken off of suicide watch, Shelly attempted to take her own life again. Sitting in the hospital, contemplating the pain that he was now re-experiencing, Jeremy wrote these words:

It was a grueling day filled with a lot of suffering, mixed with moments of pure joy. I stood on my porch overlooking the evening and actually caught myself saying, "God, thanks for giving me such a great day!" The earthly self then asked what in the world was great about it? I don't really know. It was downright miserable. Many tears were shed, many questions were asked, and many "what ifs" were thrown around. But I guess God was right there in the middle with His arms outstretched, saying "This is my beauty! This is my suffering! This is my beautiful bride of Christ!"

I used to say, "I don't wish to have any man go through what I have gone through." I'm starting to change my tune. I am tasting suffering and it is ever so sweet. God is sharing with me His pain, His power, His incredible love. I am not voyeur of His glory. Oh no, I'm taking part. I'm picking up His cross and carrying it with joy.

Jeremy had found the blessing of suffering. I'm sure it sounds contradictory to many people to think of suffering as a blessing. Most of us spend our whole lives trying to avoid it. The main thing that everyone pursues is "happiness" or what we *think* will make us happy; we certainly don't seek ways to suffer. In America, this thought is so prevalent that the "pursuit of happiness" is an unalienable right in the Declaration of Independence, the foundation of our entire country.

Many people also have the same view of God—that His main purpose is to *provide* us with happiness. We may think, "If I worship Him and do what He says, then He will bless me and I will be happy." It is a common assumption that because God is good, He blesses us with worldly happiness all of the time.

I would agree that everything He allows *is* "for the good of those who know Him and who are called according to His purpose" (Romans 8:29), but I would disagree that suffering is not a part of that plan—suffering is also used for our good, including the suffering of loneliness.

It is true that God delights in doing good things for His children. As Jesus tells us in Matthew 7:9-11, "What man is there among you who, when his son asks for a loaf, will give him a stone? Or if he asks for a fish, he will not give him a snake, will he? If you then, being evil, know how to give good gifts to your children, how much more will your Father who is in heaven give what is good to those who ask Him!"

But we are also told in Romans 8:16-17, "The Spirit Himself testifies with our spirit that we are children of God, and if children, heirs also, heirs of God and fellow heirs with Christ, *if indeed we suffer with Him so that we may also be glorified with Him*" (emphasis mine).

In his book *Praying Backwards*, Bryan Chapell explains it this way: "Prayer does not relieve all suffering, but it assures us that no difficulty comes without a purpose. When we pray 'in Jesus' name,' we have God's assurance that He will answer our prayer in a way that brings glory to Jesus and furthers His kingdom. When the Lord said of the apostle Paul, 'He must suffer for my name' the Savior was not intending to ignore the apostle's prayers but was promising to use them beyond Paul's imagining (Acts 9:16). The difficulties Paul would have been crazy to want, God used to glorify the name of Jesus throughout the world."

Christians are called to rejoice and be glad in our sufferings. In Romans 5:3-5, Paul writes, "And not only this, but we also exult in our tribulations, knowing that tribulation brings about perseverance; and perseverance, proven character; and proven character, hope; and hope does not disappoint, because the love of God has been poured out within our hearts through the Holy Spirit who was given to us." This passage (and many others) throughout the New Testament tells us that if we are believers, we *will* suffer with Christ.

The story of Joseph in the Old Testament is a perfect example of this kind of suffering. Joseph had 11 older brothers, and they hated him because he found favor in his father's eyes. As a result, the brothers sold him as a slave in Egypt, and told their father that he was dead. Years later after experiencing false accusations, prison, and other sufferings, Joseph became a ruler of Egypt. He had more power than anyone but Pharaoh, and the people loved him. At one point, the land experienced seven years of famine, but Joseph was prepared with grain stored for food. Later his brothers were forced to come to him for financial assistance. They were afraid that Joseph would take vengeance on them because of what they did to him. Instead, however, Joseph knew that God's hand had been upon his life, and he responded with these words in Genesis 50:19-20a: "Do not be afraid, for am I in God's place? As for you, you meant evil against me, *but God meant it for good...*" (emphasis mine).

Joseph saw the purpose for his suffering and God's sovereign hand, even in the midst of the hurt. Had his brothers not sold him into slavery then he would have never become ruler, and the people of Egypt would not have been saved from starvation. Joseph met his wife in Egypt; his sons were born in Egypt, and these events that took place were all due to his being sold into slavery. Even though his brothers meant their acts for evil, God's plan was for the greater good.

I grew up in a church that taught when you are *not* suffering, you are experiencing God's favor, and when you *are* suffering you are being . punished for sin or lack of faith. But the book of Job proves that theory untrue. The entire book is dedicated to the story of a man who suffered *because* he was a faithful servant of God.

In Job 1:8, God spoke to Satan saying, "Have you considered my servant Job? For there is no one like him on the earth, a blameless and upright man, fearing God and turning from evil." From there, God gave Satan the permission to cause Job every suffering, except for death. Job had a large family and he was the wealthiest man in the land, but Satan destroyed all of his possessions, killed his family members, and even struck his body with diseases, all in attempt to prove to God that Job would not be faithful to Him if all of his gifts were taken away.

But we are told, "Job did not sin with his lips" (Job 2:9-10). Even when Job's wife told him to curse God and die, Job said, "You speak as one of the foolish women speaks. Shall we indeed accept good from God and not accept adversity?"

God *chose* Job to suffer. God was the One who pointed out Job to Satan, not the other way around. Suffering did not come upon this righteous man because he was an *unfaithful* servant, but quite the contrary—because he was *faithful*. Of course, the story didn't end there. When the suffering subsided, God restored everything back to Job twofold (42:10), and Job lived another 140 years "full of his days" (42:16-17).

When I learned that suffering is not necessarily a *bad* thing, or a sign of God's disdain, my perspective of loneliness (and consequently my Christianity) was radically changed. Suddenly, my calling of loneliness was a privilege; it was a way to be like Christ, who also suffered for us, even far more than any of us could imagine.

It was this truth that sustained me through the death of my husband. If it wasn't for the hope of knowing that God was using this tragedy for good, I would not have been able to see the miracles God worked in others' lives around me. Grief can be self-absorbing because it forces a person to focus on survival, which can cause you to set aside ministering and serving others. But I concentrated on the scriptures that promised light out of darkness, pleasure out of pain, and I saw glimpses of rainbows in the midst of the storm clouds.

We can be honest about how much the wounds hurt and at the same time be thankful for all that God is doing in our lives through our loneliness. We don't have to choose one over the other. Both are true.

In my situation, the graces through my suffering came in many ways. Many wives have expressed how my loss persuaded them to love their husbands better and not take marriage for granted. A letter that my late husband wrote about his convictions regarding marriage was quoted in our state newspaper. Many wrote to express how his thoughts were challenging and moving. His words saved at least one marriage that I know of, and was read at a wedding two states away to help the young couple start out right. I have no idea how far and wide this tragedy reached people. But I do know that had David not died, the story would not have spread. Only God knows how our story has impacted other's lives.

Would I have chosen this painful road to see such graces? No, but I feel privileged to have seen life from this point of view. There are many who will never experience the kind of love I've been shown or the kind of faith it takes to walk this journey, so I'm honored to receive such gifts even at so great a cost.

In her book *Living Whole Without a Better Half* Wendy Widder wrote, "It requires great mental discipline to fight loneliness. It takes constant effort to walk closely with [God], drawing upon His companionship. It takes work to practice His presence …. In fact, God invites me to do more than 'get through' lonely times; He invites me to know Him in deeper ways, ways impossible without the pain of rejection."

Some may question that theology. How can suffering possibly be good? Is it good when someone's heart is breaking? Is it good when feelings of rejection overwhelm you so much that the tears never seem to stop flowing?

No, these situations are not good in and of themselves, but good comes from what God can use those sufferings to do in our lives. As Romans 8:29 says, "And we know that God causes *all things to work together for good* to those who love God, to those who are called according to His purpose" (emphasis mine). Suffering for the sake of suffering is not what

23

God has in mind when He allows us to sustain difficulty, but there is a *reason* why we go through it.

Mother Teresa of Calcutta said, "You can and must expect suffering. It is a sign that Jesus is near when you are suffering. Jesus is very near, watching you. Suffering empties us out for Jesus."[1]

When you understand the power of suffering, your life will radically change like mine and like my friend Claudia. Claudia had recently gone through a break-up with the love of her life, the one she thought she would marry. Being in her early 30's, she had fears of being alone forever. The girls at work were teasing her for not being sexually active and encouraged her to get another boyfriend just for fun. But Claudia knew that there was a reason for her hurt, so she wrote to me to seek counsel.

Through a series of e-mails, Claudia and I worked through her insecurities. I had the privilege of telling her about God's love for her, and teaching Claudia how to seek God's plan for her life. A month later, she was different woman. Here is an excerpt from a letter:

> *My life has changed completely. Do you remember my anguish, fears, pain, and spiritual struggles that I was going through? Well, things are different now. My soul and my heart are in the best shape they have ever been in.*
>
> *As you told me, I simply opened the Bible and started to read it, asking God for His mercy, and for the first time I understood what I read—it "clicked"! I am amazed because I am another me. I now understand that, "It is not me, but it is Christ who lives in me."*
>
> *These past two months, I thought I wanted to die, but they have been the best for my spiritual growth! I never imagined how I could change so fast—how He could transform me and get me on the path of becoming a godly woman.*

Claudia discovered what it means to exalt in her tribulations. The agony is what caused her to find her acceptance in Christ alone, and it has radically changed her life for the better. Had she not gone through this hurt, she would still be on the same dead-end road today, seeking to find her approval in a relationship. Though the suffering was a tough road, she is grateful to have traveled it.

We Need a Hero

When a person goes through a season of suffering, the pain exposes a need or desire. A pain in your stomach means you need food. A pain in your chest means a lack of blood. In the same way, the pain of loneliness shows a need for relationship. But marriage can only meet that need in so many ways. True contentment, acceptance, and love can only come through a deeper relationship with Jesus Christ—the only perfect person and the only one who can complete us.

There were many nights during my early single life after socializing with friends who were content in relationships when I couldn't wait to come home and cry. The pain of rejection was just too much to bear. Since I couldn't go into my home without disturbing my roommates, I would sit in my car, parked in front of my house, and weep. I had nowhere to go, no one to understand. Every avenue of relationship was closed … except one.

There in my car, I would look up into the dark, star-filled sky and find comfort, knowing that there was a God beyond those heavens who was so much bigger than I. There were many times when I literally felt the warmth of my Savior's loving arms around me as I wept and prayed to Him in my car.

That unlikely place became my sanctuary. I found safety in my prayer times there, and for the first time in my life I really understood what it meant to be laid bare naked spiritually before God. I had nothing to hide, no one to impress, no need to put on a happy face. I could relax in the bare honest truth—I was hurting, and Jesus completely understood my pain.

Hebrews 4:15-16 tells us, "For we do not have a High Priest [Jesus] who cannot sympathize with our weaknesses, but One who has been tempted in all things as we are, yet without sin. Therefore let us draw near with confidence to the throne of grace, so that we may receive mercy and find grace to help in time of need." Jesus can empathize with our suffering because He also suffered rejection, skepticism, mocking. He understands our weaknesses because He was tempted, just like we are. We worship a God who doesn't just look at us from afar, but came and lived this life so He could know what it is like to be us.

I started to crave my time in the car. The depth of my earthly loneliness made the comfort and acceptance I found in Christ have so

25

much more meaning, the way light blinds you when you've been in the darkness for so long. There I could confess all my hurt and pain to the One who understands. I could cry out loud, and no one would hear me but God. I could tell Him anything, and I felt His compassion for me. In my little sanctuary, I felt completely accepted, loved, and cherished, even in the midst of pain … and *because* of the pain.

As a widow I spend those times in the sanctuary of my room after the children are asleep. Whether lying in bed, sitting in my chair, or at the writing desk, that little room became my personal Holy of Holies, where I met with the presence of God. I sought Him out, asked questions, read His word, and prayed, prayed, prayed. In whispers He spoke to me, and as I moved through the grieving process He revealed each truth in His time.

It was through suffering loneliness that provided the heaviness to press me into Christ. Had I not been rained on, I would not have been driven to seek shelter. Had my heart not been broken in two, I would not have required a surgeon. Had I not been in trouble, I would not have sought a hero.

A.W. Tozer said, "It is doubtful whether God can bless a man greatly until He has hurt him deeply."[2] It was clear during my single years that I needed God's grace, but becoming a single mom showed me just how much I needed it. Parenting alone is a daunting task; it was never meant to be a one-person job. I constantly worried about my children's emotional health—were they getting all they needed? I felt the physical burden of doing *everything* by myself—the dishes, the trash, repairs, yard work—it all fell on me to care for. There were no days off, no holidays, no one to stay with the kids while I ran an errand or spent time with friends. Single parenting takes loneliness to a whole new level, not only emotionally but physically and mentally. It was spending time with my spouse that gave my heart and mind a reprieve from taking care of two toddlers all day, and when he died, that place of rest was gone.

But in Matthew 5:4, Jesus said, "*Blessed* are those who mourn, for they shall be comforted" (emphasis mine). Through the mourning, I was privileged to experience the patient love of God for me. I had many questions and fears, even of God Himself. I wondered if He still loved me. I wondered if He had removed His hand of protection and blessing from me. But in response to each violent question He had a gentle answer. The times the Holy Spirit spoke to my heart was with lovingkindness, like a caring father who had compassion for my pain but knew that this was the road that I must travel. The answers often came to my heart in almost a whisper. Who has the honor of hearing God's voice but those who have a reason to listen?

Do you have a place where you can come to Jesus in silence and solitude and let out all of your pain and hurt? I would suggest finding a room, a place on the back porch, a bench at your church, or perhaps your car. Then start a conversation with the One who understands. When you are going through a particularly difficult season, don't try to hide your suffering from God, but humbly confess your feelings, thoughts, and needs to Christ. He understands. As you begin to confide in Him, you will find that you can trust Him with your whole heart, and you will feel the healing touch of Jesus.

Learning Compassion

As you experience the healing understanding of Christ, you will begin to learn compassion for others. According to Merriam-Webster's online dictionary, compassion is a Latin word meaning "to bear suffering." And that's exactly what compassion is—to carry someone else's burden. By listening and understanding another person's problems, you give her a sense of relief, just like you feel when you confess your feelings to God.

The catch is that learning compassion can only come through suffering. We no longer just *listen* to how they feel, but we *understand* it. Personal anguish softens our hearts to the hurting and downtrodden. After having been hurt ourselves, we can see the ache in others and identify with their wounds.

Before I had truly known heartbreak, I didn't understand how others had such a hard time getting over broken relationships. I remember the first time I witnessed a girl crying after her boyfriend broke up with her. I was 10 and she was 17. I wanted to play dolls, and she just wanted to grieve. I, of course, thought it was the silliest thing I had ever witnessed—crying over a boy! After experiencing it for myself, I look back on that memory and feel sorry for her. She was crushed, and all she needed was a listening, sympathetic ear.

One of the greatest comforts to me after losing my first husband was talking to other young widows. I wanted to know how they coped with loneliness, made decisions, and found a way to live again. Because of what they went through, they could comfort me. No one else could bring

27

any relief because I knew that the others didn't understand. Only another widow could feel the depth of the wound.

Now when I see others experiencing the pain of loneliness, whether through death, divorce, or never being married, it becomes a connection that brings me closer to them. I understand what they are feeling. I have learned the meaning of Romans 12:15-16, "Weep with those who weep. Be of the same mind toward one another, do not be haughty in mind but associate with the lowly."

I'll never forget the day during my early single years when I was on the receiving end of true compassion from another person. I was particularly downhearted that day, feeling very hurt, rejected, and unwanted after my boyfriend had broken my heart. I sat alone at the kitchen table with my head buried in my arms, sobbing softly to myself. My brother Matt walked into the room and stopped behind me. I expected the same old speech—"Be glad you're rid of him; he didn't deserve you anyway …" But to my surprise, my brother gently placed his hand on my shoulder, and didn't say a word. He lifted me up, embraced me in his arms, placing his head on my shoulders, and began weeping bitterly with me. There were no words exchanged between us, only the sobs of deep sorrow.

He truly *felt* my pain that day. It was the truest sense of compassion I have ever experienced. It touched me so deeply that my eyes fill with tears even now as I write these words. His shared sorrow gave me a sense of relief, like he was helping me carry this heavy load. I felt I didn't have to go through this alone. Someone not only understood my pain, but he felt it as deeply as I did.

That experience showed me first-hand the value of compassion, but the only way anyone can have this kind of empathy is to first experience the suffering. 2 Corinthians 1:3-5 says, "Blessed be the God and Father of our Lord Jesus Christ, the Father of mercies and God of all comfort, who comforts us in all our affliction so that we will be able to comfort those who are in any affliction with the comfort with which we ourselves are comforted by God. For just as the sufferings of Christ are ours in abundance, so also our comfort is abundant through Christ."

When you see your loneliness as a way of finding empathy for others, a phenomenon takes place. Suddenly, the hurt is no longer just a burden to carry, but it becomes a tool to help you seek others whom you can *help* by lifting their load. In return, you no longer feel lonely, but instead you feel a sense of purpose that comes *through* the loneliness. As Bill Bright, founder of Campus Crusade for Christ, said, "We will never know why bad things happen, but we can discover what good things can emerge from them. Affliction is often the messenger of God's deepest truths."[3]

To experience the blessing of suffering, you must decide to be the kind of person that others can trust with their secrets and a shoulder to cry on. Be a good listener. Be willing to care and to share life with others. Remember the words of Romans 12:15: "Rejoice with those who rejoice and weep with those who weep."

Be careful, however, not to follow temptations of sins like gossip. Learning a lot of painful secrets about others could tempt a person to share that information, which often turns into dangerous rumors. A compassionate heart cares more about being a haven for the hurting than sharing the latest tidbits of information about someone else. Be the kind of friend that you desire to have, and keep confidences safe in the vault of your heart. Practice the Golden Rule, "Do unto others what you would have them to unto you."

Also, don't confuse compassion with self-pity. Having compassion is not the same as wallowing in your own sadness. Philippians 2:3-4 "Do nothing from selfish or empty conceit, but with humility of mind regard one another as more important than yourselves." Compassion is focused on others, and self-pity is focused on self. Self-pity seeks to make everyone center their affections on you, while compassion seeks to love others by listening, understanding, and carrying someone else's sorrows, setting yourself aside.

The blessings of suffering are not easy to come by, but with God's grace, you can find purpose and pleasure through your loneliness. As others share your burdens and vice versa, you will discover a greater love beyond what any relationship can give you, and one that transcends the cost of pain. Bonds with friends will grow tighter, and people will put their trust in you. As you seek others to love in this fashion, the love will be reciprocated, soothing the wounds of loneliness, and all of these will come through the blessings of suffering.

Chapter 4

The Blessings of Dying to Self

"If anyone wishes to come after Me, he must deny himself, take up his cross and follow Me. For whoever wishes to save his life will lose it; but whoever loses his life for My sake will find it"
-Matthew 16:24

During my pre-married years I attended the weekly singles service at my church, but each time I left my house to drive to the church, I shook with intimidation as I entertained the thought of seeing my ex-boyfriend. Would he be with a new girlfriend? Would he notice me? Would he finally change his mind about our relationship and come back to me? Thoughts like these consumed my mind. Once I arrived, if I saw him talking to a girl, I compared myself to her. If he acted sad, I wondered if he missed me. If he left the room, I had to know where he went.

I felt as if I was captured by an obsession I couldn't stop. He plagued my every thought. But as I began to pray for deliverance of my neurotic thinking, the Holy Spirit showed me that it wasn't a man that consumed my thoughts—it was *myself. I was really obsessed with me!*

My own insecurities kept my mind off of Christ and onto my ex-boyfriend. I was somehow convinced that if I could only persuade him to take me back, I would finally prove that I was everything I believed I was, namely a really great girl! His approval became the symbol of my accomplishment to become the perfect woman. Since my ex-boyfriend was my most critical judge, I used his opinion as the standard by which I measured my progress. As a result, I was continuously aware of myself—How was I acting? Did I look pretty enough? Who was I talking to? I wanted to be pleasing and acceptable to my ex, so that I could make up for the rejection that I felt.

Maybe you know what I mean. Your situation doesn't have to be with an ex-boyfriend. Are you ever so consumed with your own insecurities that you feel like it's all you think about? For example, when you hear someone laugh, do you automatically wonder, *Are they laughing at me?* When you see someone glance at you, is your first thought, *Are they talking about me?* Do you always feel like people are staring at you, watching you, thinking strange thoughts about you, and for some reason, you never seem good enough—always striving to be well liked and accepted?

We all have a tendency to think only about whatever is causing the greatest amount of discomfort and then disregard other areas in our lives that may need work. It's like an old joke I once heard: A man went to the doctor because his knee was hurting. He said, "Doctor, please help me stop thinking about this pain in my knee!" So the doctor stepped on his toe. "Ouch!" the man said, "What did you do that for?" To which the doctor replied, "I was trying to help you stop thinking about your knee."

If we're not careful, loneliness can become the greatest pain that causes us to think only about ourselves all the time. These thoughts can come in many different forms like: "Why don't I have someone to love?" "What can I do to improve myself so I will be wanted?"

That's where I was—overtaken by insecurity and jealousy, making it hard to think about anyone else but myself. I prayed that God would show me how to keep from being controlled by these feelings. Then He reminded me of Christ's call, "If anyone wishes to come after Me, he must deny himself, take up his cross and follow Me. For whoever wishes to save his life will lose it; but whoever loses his life for My sake will find it" (Matthew 16:24).

It was a curious thought—hadn't I already followed Him? Hadn't I accepted the cross and the kingship of Christ … or had I?

The call to take up our cross is more than just an *understanding* of what Christ did for us. It's a call to follow Christ *in His death*. It's not referring to a physical death but a death of our selfish nature, or what the

Bible calls the "old self," the person we were before we met Christ. Paul tells us in Romans 6:3-6a:

> *Do you not know that all of us who have been baptized into Christ Jesus have been baptized into His death? Therefore we have been buried with Him through baptism into death, so that as Christ was raised from the dead through the glory of the Father, so we too might walk in newness of life. For if we have become united with Him in the likeness of His death, certainly we shall also be in the likeness of His resurrection, knowing this, that our old self was crucified with Him...*

The death of our "old self" not only allows us to be resurrected with Him, it also frees us from the desires to sin. In other words, when we accept the death of our old nature, we no longer want to do things contrary to God's character. We are living *through* Christ. Paul describes it in Galatians 2:20, "I have been crucified with Christ; and it is no longer I who live, but Christ who lives in me; and the life which I now live in the flesh I live by faith in the Son of God, who loved me and gave Himself up for me." We die to all the sins of the old nature, including the sin of self-focus.

I began to picture my physical body like a shell. Inside the shell, my old nature was a balloon, and when I popped the balloon, it withered away. Then I pictured Christ's form taking up the space that my 'self' once occupied. Now my body is no longer controlled by my old nature, but it is controlled by Christ who is living *in* me. Dying to self actually frees us up to be an empty vessel, filled with Christ, and used to do His will.

Bill Bright said in his book *His Intimate Presence*:

> *The truth of Scripture reminds me that I am crucified, dead, buried, and raised to newness of life with Christ (Romans 6). My flesh, the old Bill Bright, is at war with God. It never did please God and never will (Romans 8:7).*
>
> *In many words and ways, I daily acknowledge (according to these wonderful truths as well as Colossians 3 and other passages) that the old Bill Bright is dead and should have as little desire for this world as a dead man. I am alive to Christ, a suit of*

clothes for Him. I invite Him, in all of His resurrection love and power, to control my thoughts, desires, attitudes, actions, and words.

When we leave our old self in the grave, then Christ fills up our "suit" as Bright calls it, and we are free from the controlling thoughts and feelings of the sinful nature. It isn't that we physically die in that moment, but our lives reflect new life, a life that by its nature—a new nature— desires the will of God. Romans 12:1-2 describes this as becoming a "living sacrifice."

Therefore I urge you, brethren, by the mercies of God, to present your bodies a living and holy sacrifice, acceptable to God, which is your spiritual service of worship. And do not be conformed to this world, but be transformed by the renewing of your mind, so that you may prove what the will of God is, that which is good and acceptable and perfect.

In this verse, to sacrifice means "to kill or to slaughter *for a purpose.*" We are not dying for the sake of simply ending the life we've come to know, but on the contrary, we are dying so that we may *have* life— abundant life! Before we knew Christ, we were living in bodies that were destined for eternal death. There was no life in us. But when Christ took control of our lives and we were born again, He breathed into us His life, just as God breathed life into Adam (Genesis 2:7).

In my experience, remembering the death of myself helped me overcome the thoughts of relationships that plagued my mind, and I was outwardly able to control my emotions. When rising fear, jealousy, and panic came, I would shut my eyes and imagine myself being crucified. When that wasn't enough to help, I would literally physically throw my hands out like a cross, look up toward heaven, and focus on the living, breathing all-powerful Christ who gives me strength in times of need. You see, dying to self is not as much about your own death as it is about finding life in Christ.

It is important to realize that dying to self is an action that takes place day by day. Jesus commands us in Luke 9:23 to pick up the cross *daily*. John Piper wrote, "Daily Christian living is daily Christian dying. The dying I have in mind is the dying of comfort and security and reputation and health and family and friends and wealth and homeland. These may be taken from us at any time in the path of Christ-exalting obedience. To die daily the way Paul did, and to take up our cross daily the way Jesus commanded, is to embrace this life of loss for Christ's sake and count it gain." [4]

Never have I understood this more clearly than when David died. He was the one I leaned on for security. Since I was a stay-at-home mom, I depended on him financially and to help me take care of the children. He was my lover, so I depended on him for emotional needs, like affection and acceptance. He was my best friend, so I depended on him for encouragement and entertainment. One of the blessings I received during my loneliness as a widow was seeing how God provides each and every one of these needs. It certainly wasn't without tears as I battled my way through dying to self, but I continually saw how God gave me life in the midst of my darkest hours.

For singles the dying of comfort, security, and reputation usually means the death of exalting marriage before Christ. When I learned as a young single woman what it meant to carry my cross, I walked in the mindset that I was dead and only Christ lived through me. It no longer mattered what my ex-boyfriend thought of me because, that old girl he dated? "She died, remember?" I would remind myself. It no longer mattered about how pretty or nice his new girlfriend was; there was no need for jealousy if the old self was dead—Jesus was now living in my place, and He is perfect and complete. I had everything I needed within me.

The most wonderful part about being "dead" was that it allowed me to concentrate on others. Nancy Leigh DeMoss wrote, "I believe one of the reasons that so many people live with chronic loneliness is that they are unwilling to die … When we refuse to shed that hard, outer shell called *self*, no one can get close to us; no one can penetrate or enter into our life." [5]

When I was "dead" I could ask questions and love people without fear of what they thought about me. I could get close to them and them to me. All at once, *I* wasn't the most important thing in my life anymore. As a matter of fact, I was nothing. With my own agenda out of the way, the love of Christ flowed through me generously without fear of scrutiny. The shackles I had put on myself fell off and I was free! The jealousy left me. The insecurities left me. The thoughts of the inadequacies that plagued me left, and there was nothing to think about but Christ and loving others.

One of my favorite passages is from the book *Hinds Feet in High Places* by Hannah Hurnard, in which this kind of self-giving death is described in the vision of a waterfall. The main character of the book, Much-Afraid (a name that reflects man's true nature), has been taken on a journey guided by the Shepherd (the symbol of Jesus).[6]

> *There stood Much-Afraid, a tiny figure at the foot of the mighty cliffs, looking up at the great, never-ending rush of waters as they cast themselves down from the High Places. She thought that never before had she seen anything so majestic or so terrifyingly lovely. The height of the rocky lip, over which the waters cast themselves to be dashed in pieces the rocks below, almost terrified her. At the foot of the fall, the thunderous voice of the waters seemed almost deafening, but it seemed also to be filled with meaning, grand and awesome, beautiful beyond expression.*

As Much-Afraid listened, she heard the waters singing:

> *"From the heights we leap and go
> To the valleys down below,
> Always answering to the call,
> To the lowest place of all."*
>
> *"Much-Afraid," said the Shepherd's voice in her ear, "what do you think of this fall of great waters in their abandonment of self-giving?"*
>
> *She trembled a little as she answered. "I think they are beautiful and terrible beyond anything which I ever saw before."*
>
> *"Why so terrible?" he asked.*
>
> *"It is the leap which they have to make, the awful height from which they must cast themselves down to the depths beneath, there to be broken on the rocks. I can hardly bear to watch it."*
>
> *"Look closer," he said again. "Let your eye follow just one part of the water from the moment when it leaps over the edge until it reaches the bottom."*
>
> *Much-Afraid did so, and then almost gasped with wonder. Once over the edge, the waters were like winged things, alive with joy, so utterly abandoned to the ecstasy of giving themselves that Much-Afraid could almost have supposed that she was looking at a*

36

*host of angels floating down on rainbow wings, singing with
rapture as they went.*

*She gazed and gazed, then said, "It looks as though they think it
is the loveliest movement in all the world, as though to cast oneself
down is to abandon oneself to ecstasy and joy indescribable…"*

*"…At first sight perhaps the leap does look terrible," said the
Shepherd, "but as you can see, the water itself finds no terror in it,
no moment of hesitation or shrinking, only joy unspeakable, and
full of glory, because it is the movement natural to it. Self-giving is
its life. It has only one desire, to go down and down and give itself
with no reserve or holding back of any kind. You can see that as it
obeys that glorious urge the obstacles which look so terrifying are
perfectly harmless, and indeed only add to the joy and glory of the
movement."*

At first, Much Afraid saw the self-giving of the waters as terrifying,
but looking closer, she saw the joy within the casting down of their lives,
and she admired the glory of it. Just like the waters that Much-Afraid saw
dashing themselves upon the rock, we, too, can experience the joy and
ecstasy of giving of ourselves, as we rush to die.

The Bible promises that those who give their lives for the sake of
Christ will find life in return (Luke 9:24). Jesus used the example of a
seed to explain how life comes from death. If a seed were to remain alive,
it would never fulfill its purpose, but when a seed dies and is planted, it
produces life. In John 12:24-25, Jesus says:

> *Truly, truly, I say to you, unless a grain of wheat falls into the
> earth and dies, it remains alone; but if it dies, it bears much fruit.
> He who loves his life loses it, and he who hates his life in this
> world will keep it to life eternal.*

Each of us is a seed, but most of us try so hard to keep from dying.
We want our way. We don't want to sacrifice our dreams and goals to
accomplish the will of God, especially not the timing and details of dating
and marriage. We want to be in control of our own lives. We think we
know what's best, and the more we try to stay alive, the more we are
forced to pay attention to ourselves. It takes a lot of concentration on your

ego to stay alive—you need the life-giving components of on-going compliments, affection, and attention.

But if we could let go of tending to our own soulful needs, let go of putting our energies toward our own nourishment, then we, the seeds, would dry out and die, and as a result, we would produce fruit, like love, joy, peace, patience, kindness, goodness, faithfulness, gentleness, and self-control.

On the contrary, if we cling to the old life, we will not find our true God-given purpose, and produce nothing. In his book *Don't Waste Your Life*, Piper writes, "I believe one of the reasons so many people live with chronic loneliness is that they are unwilling to die. As Jesus pointed out, if a grain of wheat does not fall into the ground and die, it 'remains alone.'"

In my life, the fruit of my death as I dealt with loneliness allowed me to minister to other women. Since I was no longer afraid of rejection, I could honestly confess my faults, and in return, they weren't afraid to admit their struggles to me. I became a sounding board and often a mentor based on what God had done for me—all of this because of the lessons that I learned through my own death.

After the passing of my first husband, these lessons came flooding back to me. It was a great comfort knowing that my experience would help me identify with a whole new set of people that I never would otherwise comprehend fully, such as, single parents, other widows, and even divorcees who had been abandoned by their spouses.

Believe me, this was not the life I wanted! When my husband died, my dreams were shattered. Not only did the experience require dying to self in a spiritual sense, my entire future died with him. But as I struggled through the meaning of it all, it came back to me over and over that my story would be useful to bring comfort to others and ultimately to share the Gospel. If only one person comes to have eternal salvation, then the darkest depths of loneliness were worth the price.

Learning to Die

The battle between the flesh (the old self) and the spirit (the new self) is not easily won. All of us will have a tug of war with spiritual and carnal desires every day. Even the Apostle Paul saw the battle between the spirit and the flesh in his own life as he describes in Romans 7:18-25.

For I know that nothing good dwells in me, that is, in my flesh; for the willing is present in me, but the doing of the good is not. For the good that I want, I do not do, but I practice the very evil that I do not want. But if I am doing the very thing I do not want, I am no longer the one doing it, but sin which dwells in me. I find then the principle that evil is present in me, the one who wants to do good. For I joyfully concur with the law of God in the inner man, but I see a different law in the members of my body, waging war against the law of my mind and making me a prisoner of the law of sin which is in my members. Wretched man that I am. Who will set me free from the body of this death? Thanks be to God through Jesus Christ our Lord! So then, on the one hand I myself with my mind am serving the law of God, but on the other, with my flesh the law of sin.

When facing death of the carnal, our natural tendency is to resist. We don't want to suffer; we don't want to go through pain; we don't want to let go of plans, even such wonderful, God-ordained goals such as marriage. But as a Christian you must sacrifice your own desires. Don't run from it. As Nancy Leigh DeMoss once said, "Allow [loneliness] to press you toward God."

That's not to say that we Christians shouldn't have dreams and hopes for the future. I certainly hope it is in God's plan for me to get married again. The point is not to stop wanting, but to want most the will of the Father.

In her book *Loneliness*, Elisabeth Elliot wrote, "With what misgivings we turn over our lives to God, imagining somehow that we are about to lose everything that matters. Our hesitancy is like that of a tiny shell on the seashore, afraid to give up the teaspoonful of water it holds lest there not be enough in the ocean to fill it again." Why is it that we aren't willing to give up the little that we have to receive all of the abundance of the life of Christ? Do we really believe that marriage to just any person is better than the time of singleness that God has for us? I can tell you as I've talked with many unhappily married people after eight years in full-time marriage ministry with Cru's FamilyLife ministries, it is not.

As with everything, let us turn to Jesus as our example of how to receive death. When He was in the Garden of Gethsemane on the night he was arrested, Jesus prayed, "My Father, if it is possible, let this cup pass from Me." But He didn't stop there—He added, "Yet not as I will, but as You will" (Matthew 26:39). Jesus didn't have to go through this death; He could have saved Himself (Matthew 4:6), but He chose the will of God over His own life for the sake of others.

Jesus knew that death could not hold Him. He knew He would rise from the grave, and not only would His life be restored in greater glory, but sin and death would be conquered (Hebrews 2:14). You and I have been promised the same life. Look into your heart and depend on your God-given faith to believe He will restore your joy as you accept death, not your physical death but that of your will, and depend completely upon His.

The Promise of Life

Remember, we are not called to die for the sake of death, but we are called to die in exchange for life! (John 12:25). Christ *lives* in us! And when we allow ourselves to be His empty vessel, to give up the right to control our own destinies, then we are able to take on *His* love for others, *His* compassion, *His* joy, *His* peace, and *His* satisfaction.

During the times when I allowed Christ to live through me, I was more joyful, loving, peaceful, and grateful for all that God was doing through me than I have ever been. For the first time in my life, I wasn't burdened with the cares of what others thought of me. I knew I was whole and complete through Christ, and opinions didn't matter because I realized the old Sabrina was out of the picture.

If we empty ourselves, the way Christ emptied Himself for us (Philippians 2:1-11), then all of the time we used to spend thinking of ourselves and our future, we can dedicate to giving of ourselves, loving others, ministering the greatest message of all time to everyone we meet. At that point, the pain of loneliness becomes a tool, a reminder to die, and instead of being consumed with our own pain, it makes us have thoughts like, "I wonder how Jennifer is doing today? She sometimes gets lonely, too. I think I'll call her for coffee and make sure she's okay."

In return for regarding yourself as dust and focusing completely on others, you will find love reciprocated in ways you have never known. At a leadership training conference at Willow Creek, Erwin McManus, the lead pastor and cultural architect of Mosaic church in Los Angeles, Calif., said, "The key to brokenness is not to *receive* love, but the path to wellness and whole being is to *give love away*." In other words, when you give love, you will always receive love in return, not because you demanded it but because you provided it.

Those who live this kind of others-centered single life will feel more appreciation and acceptance than any married person who is in a relationship to feed his own emotional needs. Marriage based on a person (or two people) who are self-centered are the ones experiencing an even greater loneliness. A single life doesn't mean it has to be a love-less one.

Just before I got married the first time, some close friends threw a surprise birthday party for me. To my astonishment, almost 70 people came—they were friends from church and Bible study classes, pastors, and a few family members. I have never felt more honored and encouraged in my life. It wasn't because I was such a wonderful person— I've had my share of disagreements and trials. But God had taught me to be an empty funnel, which channeled His love to them, and they were responding to the love of God that they felt through me.

There were many gifts and cards, and I shed lots of tears, but my prized possession from that event was a scrapbook full of letters of thanks and encouragement, documenting the love they wanted to share with me.

I cannot take credit for the affection I felt that day. All I did was to recognize my own death. *Christ* is the One that loved them *through* me. It has truly been one of the greatest expressions of endearment I have ever experienced.

Practical Death

So how does this death look, practically? How does one allow her self-will to die in light of Christ?

First, you must recognize and confess that you are trying to determine your path in life on your own. The purpose of confession is not to tell God what you have done. He is all-knowing and all-present, so He already knows your struggles. The purpose of confession is really an exercise in humility, and it brings out the truth in your own heart. Living life on your own, following your own desires and not God's, is part of the sin nature. If you're living that kind of lifestyle, there are telltale signs to watch for. Here are four questions to ask yourself:

- Am I consumed with my own emotional pain?
- Do I think of myself and my desires more often than others?
- Am I easily offended?
- Do I feel insecure about myself?
- Do I worry about what others think of me most of the time?

If the answer is yes to any of these four questions, then it's a good indicator that you need to die to self. Romans 8:12-13 tells us, "So then, brethren, we are under obligation, not to the flesh—for if you are living according to the flesh, you must die; but if by the Spirit you are putting to death the deeds of the body, you will live."

People spend time thinking about what is most important to them. If you spend the majority of your time thinking about yourself, then you need to reevaluate your priorities. Consuming thoughts don't necessarily mean you are being haughty, which is thinking more highly of yourself. Most of the time, actually, a person who is consumed with self feels negative feelings of self-worth, and the reason they are so consuming is because the person feels vulnerable.

But when you learn to die to the flesh, Christ becomes the greatest thought in your mind. Your love focuses on others, and you don't worry about your own emotional needs. The worth that you crave comes from Christ, and the vulnerability fades because you no longer need to protect yourself—the shadow of God's wing shelters you.

After confession, ask God to forgive your selfishness and to fill your heart with His desires, His thoughts, and His purposes.

Second, memorize this scripture: "I have been crucified with Christ; and it is no longer I who live, but Christ lives in me; and the life which I now live in the flesh I live by faith in the Son of God, who loved me and gave Himself up for me" (Galatians 2:20). Dying to self is something that happens on a continual basis. Every day, sometimes even moment by moment, I must remind myself that my old nature is dead. The battle between the spirit and the flesh rages within me, but the spirit is destined to win. Ephesians 6:17 tells us that the word of God is the sword of the spirit; it is our weapon to use within the battle. Take up your armor by memorizing scriptures, starting with Galatians 2:20.

King David, the writer of Psalms, wrote that he hid God's word in his heart so that he might not sin against Him (Psalm 40:8). The word of God has the power to save us and to strengthen us as we face temptation. Keep

His word close to your heart, and have it available when you are challenged with areas of your life that need to be removed. Hebrews 4:12 says, "For the word of God is living and active and sharper than any two-edged sword, and piercing as far as the division of soul and spirit, of both joints and marrow, and able to judge the thoughts and intentions of the heart." With such a war taking place, you need a weapon as powerful as this, ready to help you slay sin and self-centeredness at any moment.

Third, purposely focus on others. Part of dying means that you no longer worry about meeting your own emotional needs, but instead seek to meet the needs of others. A physically dead person doesn't need to eat or drink, just like a person who is dying to self needs no food for her ego or drink to nurse her insecurities. When you set your purpose to put your attention on others, then you are providing encouragement and acceptance for their wounds, leaving no room for your own. You don't have the pressure of impressing anyone or thinking of the right thing to say. You don't have to worry whether or not people like you. You have essentially made yourself an empty vessel to be used as God sees fit at that moment, placing all of your focus on the person that you are talking to.

This type of selfless behavior is really an act of love as you seek to care about others more than yourself. Jesus said that the greatest commandment is to love God with all your heart, mind, soul, and strength, and the second is like the first—to love your neighbor as you love yourself (Matthew 22:37-40). When Jesus says you are to love "as you love yourself," that does not mean that you are to put attention on yourself so that you can love others better. It means quite the opposite—that we should love our neighbor as if that person were inside our own bodies—listening to her, nurturing her, meeting her needs.

As a single person, especially one who has no children, you may not realize it, but you have the free time and flexibility to sharply focus on this kind of loving attention to others. It's a special time in life to be able to meet the needs of your brothers and sisters in Christ, whether they need a listening ear, or more practical help like someone to help move residences. The possibilities of service are endless.

First Corinthians 13 is an entire chapter of the Bible dedicated to defining love. Look at this definition from verses 4-7:

> *Love is patient, love is kind and is not jealous; love does not brag*
> *and is not arrogant, does not act unbecomingly; it does not seek its*
> *own, is not provoked, does not take into account a wrong suffered,*

43

does not rejoice in unrighteousness, but rejoices with the truth; bears all things, believes all things, hopes all things, endures all things.

All of us have emotional needs that long to be met. We want to feel like what we have to offer the world has worth, or that our stories are interesting, or that our attributes have value. When you take the time to focus on another person, you are really saying to her, "You are important to me, and it's worth my time to invest in you."

I found that one of the best ways to show this kind of affection for others is to ask questions. This simple act kept me from talking about myself all the time and helped me put my center of attention on others. Proverbs 10:19 says, "When there are many words, transgression is unavoidable, but he who restrains his lips is wise." When you ask questions about who someone is, it allows the other person time to talk, and it shows that you're interested not only in what they have to say but also in whom they are as a person. Asking questions allows you to listen; it gives you something to talk about and helps you get to know other people. Here are some examples of conversation starters:

- What do you do for a living? What do you enjoy most about your job?
- Have you lived here long? If not, where are you from and how did you come to live here? If so, tell me about your family.
- What do you like to do in your spare time?
- Where are you spiritually?

This last question has really been interesting. It often allowed me to delve into spiritual matters without coming on too strong. I got this idea after hearing Bill Bright speak on the power of the gospel. In his presentation, he explained that when he met a stranger, he would simply ask, "Where are you spiritually?" And following up with, "Have you heard the wonderful news of Jesus Christ?" As a result he led unmeasured numbers of people to Christ, including a taxi cab driver and a stranger he met in an elevator.

By asking this question I have also had the opportunity to encourage people in their growing walk with Christ. If the person was already a believer, my query would open up a faucet of fellowship between us, resulting in conversations that were inspiring and God-honoring in nature, as opposed to the surface chatter that revolve around basic topics like occupation and hobbies.

When talking to people, look them in the eyes as you interact. In our fast-paced society with all its bells and whistles and distractions, it's not easy to actually pay attention when someone is conversing. During your next conversation, notice how many times you are distracted during the exchange. Eye contact and concentration are not as easy as they sound.

Discipline yourself to notice facial expressions and listen to the tone of the person's voice. All of these things are signals that tell you about one's personality, background, and issues that they are currently dealing with. As you key in on areas of struggle, find ways to minister the healing words of encouragement from God's word, or use practical proverbs from scripture to help. The Body of Christ was designed to work in a way that comes to the aid of each member. Sometimes all it takes to be a good spiritual EMT are clear ears and sharp eyes.

Don't Give Up

Remember, dying to self is not easy. That's the reason it's referred to so often as a battle. I'm certainly no expert on winning streaks, but I am an expert on the struggle. I have to fight self-focused thoughts constantly—just tonight, I was so busy thinking about what I had to do when I got home that I zoned out of a conversation with a friend and realized I missed half of the details of her story! I felt terrible when I had to ask her to catch me up on everything she just said.

The key is not to give up on the war. Dying to self is where we find freedom from the bondages of worry, fear, purposeless, and depression. We may not win all the battles, but there will be victories, and the more we fight to suppress the self-centered nature of man, the more victories we will have.

In the battleground of loneliness, there are so many opportunities to sulk and wallow in self-pity. It can be a self-perpetuating cycle of loneliness that drives you further and further away from people. Self-pity often turns to insecurity, and insecurity can turn to bitterness and a resolve to never experience hurt. It's that resolve that makes a person build walls around her heart, keeping bitterness in and love out.

Don't let loneliness keep you alive in prison walls of isolation and bitterness. Instead, pick up your cross and follow Christ into His death, and you too can have life more real than what you could imagine—a single existence, what the world might call lonely, but full of love.

Chapter 5

The Blessings of Sacrifice

"Without faith it is impossible to please God."
-Hebrews 11:6

.

Janice was ready to get married. All of her friends were in a relationship and she felt it was time for her, as well. So she jumped into the first relationship that showed signs of ending in marriage. The problem, however, was that Janice wasn't jumping into the relationship because she felt like it was God's will for her life; she was jumping in based on her own desires to escape loneliness. The idea of marriage became a higher priority than fulfilling God's promises, so when Janice found out that the man she was preparing to marry was not a believer in Jesus Christ, she tried to justify her actions in her heart. Janice later admitted that she ignored all the warning signs that should have told her this relationship was not what God wanted for her life.

She became a very proud individual, not willing to admit that she should not continue in this romantic endeavor. "I turned my back on God," she later said, "and my heart continued to grow harder and harder toward His soft voice as I continued on in my sin."

Janice thought marriage would fulfill her, even if it were to a person who was not a Christian. During the course of their relationship, her plan was to justify her actions by trying to make the man she fell in love with fit into the mold of what she wanted her life to be. She attempted to convert her boyfriend to Christianity by witnessing regularly, but it didn't work, and yet she still tightly gripped the romance somehow convinced that there was a way that it would work out and bring her happiness; although, it did not.

Janice is not the only girl who has mistakenly believed this. Throughout my life, I met and sometimes advised dozens of single girls like Janice, who all seemed to have one thought in common—if I find a man, I'll be happy. They spend the majority of their time and energy meeting guys, always looking, always wondering, "Will this be the one?" It's a preoccupation that controls their every emotion—happy when they are in a relationship, and depressed when they are not.

Marriage is Not the Key to Happiness

Many singles believe that the answer to loneliness, and therefore the key to happiness, is marriage. They often see marriage as the ideal or perfect life. These individuals see marriage as a staple of life and find it hard to move on with the future until they find their match. Andrew Farmer, author of *The Rich Single Life*, wrote, "Many, if not most, single people still see marriage as by far the socially superior state of life. For them, singleness is a place, but marriage is the destination."

So the lonely single girl finds a man whom she thinks is appealing, and then gets married based on mutual attraction. At that point, the bride and groom think everything is supposed to be "happy." It's the Cinderella-story syndrome: When you find Prince Charming, you'll live "happily ever after."

Hear me when I say marriage does not cure loneliness. When a man or woman marries someone just to keep from being lonely, then what that person will end up with is a marriage that was built on a faulty foundation, instead of one built on trust, common goals, and spiritual strength. There are many married women and men in this world that are facing a loneliness much deeper and more hurtful than anything an unmarried person could imagine.

Marriage wasn't meant to fulfill us. God did not promise us that everyone would be married, and He didn't say that there is something wrong with those who are not married. As a matter of fact, I think you will be surprised by what the Bible does say about singleness. Let me

49

share with you two reasons why I think the "Cinderella" idea of marriage is phony.

First, Prince Charming is just a frog and so are you. I used to have a key chain that read, "You have to kiss a lot of frogs before you find your prince." But now having been married, I believe it's the other way around—you have to kiss a lot of princes to find the right frog. Singles do their best to look and act in their most attractive manner, even sometimes living or acting in ways to trick others into thinking they're something far better than what they are.

After the wedding, however, people start to reveal their leathery skin, long slimy tongues, and ugly warts. It's not that the bride and groom are changing but rather revealing the nature of their true humanity. Whether we like it or not, we're all frogs—warts and all—because none of us are perfect, and the imperfections in our own lives look just as ugly to others as theirs look to us.

There's nothing wrong with being married to a frog—all of us struggle with our warts. The problems come when we expect the frog we married to treat us like the princes or princesses we thought they were. Matrimony takes a lot of work and a lot of grace, so if you marry someone thinking he will make you happy, you are doing it for the wrong reason. In return, you will be more alone than you ever were as a single.

For example, a couple went through premarital counseling at their church. When it was finished, their counselor requested that they put off their wedding a little longer in order to give them time to work out their issues. My friends were too eager, however, to prolong their expected happiness. So they decided to ignore the counselor's advice and get married as soon as possible.

They were determined that marriage would simply iron out their problems. Only weeks after their wedding, this young lady was at my house crying, wondering if she had done the wrong thing. I reminded her of the vows she had made and sent her home, but she and her new husband had a long way to go to build a healthy foundation.

Another young lady did not experience the same happy ending. Because many of her friends were entering marriage, she felt left out and was pressured to join the crowd. She found someone attractive and agreed to marry him less than three months after their initial meeting. Even though the counselors gave them advice not to go through with their marriage immediately, they took their vows anyway. Their differences began to create problems within the first week, and right away they began counseling. After countless separations, counseling sessions, and emotional breakdowns, they divorced, leaving deep scars in their lives.

What caused these two women to decide to get married? It wasn't because they listened to wise counsel. It wasn't because they didn't have problems—both of them knew about their issues before they ever decided to say "I do." They both got married because they thought the relationship would make them happy. They saw that many of their friends had seemingly found a prince, and they wanted that, too.

Marriage is a Calling

I'm not saying that singles shouldn't want to get married. I'm not even saying that people can't be happy if they *are* married, but I am saying that marriage is a calling. The purpose of marriage is *to spend your life serving another person*. If you go into marriage without having the clear calling to accomplish that purpose, then it is better not to get married at all. Ephesians 5:22-33 tells us that the relationship between a husband and wife is a reflection of how Christ loves the church, and that kind of relationship requires that the two treat each other in a way that reflects that love. It's a sacrifice—just like Christ sacrificed Himself for His bride, the church. "As the church is subject to Christ, so also the wives ought to be to their husbands in everything. Husbands, love your wives, just as Christ also loves the church and gave Himself up for her" (Ephesians 5:24-25).

Things get complicated when you try to form two lives into one. It's not as simple as just signing a marriage license. It is better to wait for marriage until you're sure that the person you are dating is the one you are called to *serve*.

Secondly, *the idea that marriage will fulfill you is unbiblical.* Singleness is encouraged in the Bible. The most obvious example is Jesus Christ Himself, who was unmarried, yet He was perfect and complete (Hebrews 4:15).

Jesus said in Matthew 19 that if a man can accept a life as a eunuch (a person who is not sexually active), then that person should remain as he is. He says to the disciples, "Not all men can accept this statement [it is better not to marry], but only those whom it has been given. For there are eunuchs who were born that way from their mother's womb; and there are eunuchs who were made eunuchs by men; and there are also eunuchs who made themselves eunuchs for the sake of the kingdom of heaven. He who is able to accept this, let him accept it" (vs. 11-13).

The Apostle Paul echoes this advice in 1 Corinthians 7:

> *But I say to the unmarried and to widows that it is good for them if they remain even as I. But if they do not have self-control, let them marry; for it is better to marry than to burn with passion (v. 8-9).*

> *Now concerning virgins, I have no command of the Lord, but I give an opinion as one who by the mercy of the Lord is trustworthy. I think it is good in view of the present distress, that it is good for a man to remain as he is. Are you bound to a wife? Do not seek to be released. Are you released from a wife? Do not seek a wife. But if you marry, you have not sinned; and if a virgin marries, she has not sinned. Yet such will have trouble in this life, and I am trying to spare you (25-28).*

> *But I want you to be free from concern. One who is unmarried is concerned about the things of the Lord, how he may please the Lord; but one who is married, is concerned about the things of the world, how he may please his wife, and his interests are divided. The woman who is unmarried, and the virgin, is concerned about the things of the Lord, that she may be holy both in body and spirit; but one who is married is concerned about the things of the world, how she may please her husband" (v. 32-34).*

What Paul is telling us in these passages is that being single avails you to concentrate completely on God. It takes away the distraction of a husband or a wife and allows you to dedicate yourself to the cause of Christ.

As a single woman without children, I had more time to spend in the word of God, developing a deeper relationship with Him, and I had more time for others. I was able to take advantage of these opportunities, and as a result, reach more singles for Christ and help them grow spiritually.

That is not to say that once a person gets married, then she is no longer able to serve the Lord, but it is true that responsibilities at home have greater ties than before. As a wife and mother, your primary ministry is to your husband and your children.

My single friend Tammy benefited from her single years in many ways, but what I most admire are her trips with the organization Youth With a Mission (YWAM). She has been to countries all over the world, including Turkey, Egypt, Syria, Jordan, and the Ukraine. She has lead others to Christ and been a part of the Great Commission. If Tammy had married when I did, she might never have had these opportunities.

Although Tammy still feels the pains of loneliness, these experiences are worth her single status. She is willing to wait for the right man, if that is God's will, but more importantly, she is even willing to be alone for the rest of her life if God calls her to do so. Marriage is definitely her desire, and at times the singleness is hard to bear, but she continues to concentrate on the kingdom, not the aisle. Tammy embraces the pain of loneliness, instead of trying to cure it. She chooses to trust God with her future, instead of trusting a groom. Whether her future includes a mate or not, she has embraced Christ as her Prince. Seeking His will is worth the consequences, even if it means she must sacrifice her dreams of marriage and endure the pain.

Marriage: The Idol

Marriage can become an idol, taking precedence over God and His will for your life. Many singles think about marriage continuously. Even if it's not on the forefront of their daily activities, it's always in the back of their minds. Each time they meet someone of the opposite sex, they wonder, *Will this be the one?* The lonely single becomes a treasure-hunter at every social event. She feels competition toward everyone in the room, as she puts on her "game face" in order to be attractive. Perhaps it affects other areas of life in an attempt to always look her best—obsessive exercise, under-eating, frivolous spending on clothing, expensive cars—all in an attempt to win someone over. With the onslaught of online dating, this mentality receives instant gratification. Now the lonely single has a whole *world* of singles with whom she can connect and possibly choose her mate.

In all of these cases, she has become the pursuer of her own destiny— she will stop at nothing to catch the right one. But where is the pursuit of God in all of these things? He's taken a back seat to the obsession with finding a mate. Instead of trusting Him with her life and her future, she has decided to take matters into her own hands and hunt the prize.

But singles who live this way are missing out on the pleasure of waiting on God. I like the illustration by Tommy Nelson, pastor of Denton Bible Church in Denton, Texas, and author of the Song of Solomon series. In his messages, Nelson describes finding a mate in terms of a race. All of us as Christians are running toward a goal—not marriage but Christ. Nelson suggests to singles that when you are well into a steady pace, look beside you and see who is running next to you. Then link arms with that person. That's the one you should marry. He encourages singles not to try to catch up with someone because you will never be able to keep up the pace long-term, and not to slow down to be with someone because his or her slow pace will eventually disappoint you and later frustrate you. But he suggests keeping your eyes on the goal—Christ, not the other runners. So what do you do if there is no one next to you? Just keep running toward the goal.

By keeping your goal as Christ and not marriage, you will always be headed in the right direction. Have you ever been driving when you were distracted by something on the side of the road? You look toward the object that has captured your attention, and the longer you stare, the further you drift in that direction. It's the same thing in our race towards Christ. If you keep your eye on the goal, you will make it to the finish line, and even though you may be running the race alone for a while (and possibly for your entire life) you will find that sense of purpose and accomplishment as you come closer to the end.

How to Sacrifice Marriage

Have you come to the place where you are willing to sacrifice your dreams of marriage? Here are some questions to help you evaluate:

- Do you think about marriage all of the time?
- Do you feel like your life is on hold until you find a mate?
- Does the hope of marriage weigh in your decision-making for the future?
- Are you willing to sacrifice your standards for a potential mate in order to get married?

If you answered yes to any of these questions, then you need to ask God to change your heart, and let Him take control of your life. By keeping marriage as the main goal, you may be missing out on opportunities God has set before you. Stop pursuing people, and start racing toward Jesus. Here's is how to rest in trusting God to control your destiny.

First, strengthen your faith in Christ. Hebrews 11:1 tells us that "faith is the assurance of things hoped for, the conviction of things not seen." In other words, faith means acting upon something that you know exists even if you can't see it. One of the best images of faith in action comes from the movie *Indiana Jones and the Last Crusade*. In the movie, Jones must go through a series of tests in order to obtain the Holy Grail. In one of the tests, he must take a "leap of faith" across a great chasm. The leap is too far for any human to successfully make, but there is apparently no bridge or any way to cross. So Jones closes his eyes, takes a deep breath, and steps out into the air, hoping for a miracle. Amazingly, his foot hits a solid substance, and there before him lies a bridge, which had been camouflaged into the wall by an optical illusion. The only way he could have found the bridge was to *first* step on it.

The same is true for the Christian life. Oftentimes God calls us to do things that may seem impossible—even sacrificial—but if we will only obey Him, despite our fears, then He will make the way clear. The Bible tells us in Hebrews 11:6 that "without faith it is impossible to please God," but that is not the end of the statement. It goes on to say, "for he who comes to God must believe that He is [exists] and that He is the *rewarder of those who seek Him*" (emphasis mine). Part of faith requires that we believe that these hardships we face while seeking Him will lead to great rewards—even when we endure hardships like loneliness. Although these blessings are not promised as earthly goods, their measure is too great to compare. They come in intangible forms, like peace, contentment, and everlasting life.

Understanding the nature of faith is only part of strengthening it; next you must learn *how* to strengthen it. Romans 10:17 tells us "faith comes by hearing and hearing by the word of God." God's promise is clear—the more you hear and read the words of the Bible, the more your faith will grow. As you feed on God's word you will not only understand His message, but you will get to know Jesus, who is the "author and perfecter of our faith" (Hebrews 12:2).

Consuming God's word is not merely a matter of knowledge because "knowledge makes arrogant" (1 Corinthians 8:1), but it's a matter of sustenance. As Christ reminds us in Matthew 4:4, "Man shall not live on bread alone, but on every word that proceeds out of the mouth of God." Just as your body needs food on a consistent basis, your spirit needs the word of God to be nourished. Feed your faith.

When Jesus was being tempted in the wilderness, He responded to each of Satan's three temptations with scripture. Each response began with the words, "It is written..." (Matthew 4:4, 7, and 10). I found that the same was true when experiencing loneliness. The temptation to feel sorry for myself and feel like no one loved me was difficult to resist, but by memorizing the word of God, I was reminded that God loved me (John 3:16), He has overcome the world (John 16:33), and He will never leave me alone (Matthew 28:20). During my times of extreme feelings of isolation, the scriptures I had memorized were of great comfort to me, many of which I have shared in this book.

If memorization is a chore for you, write scriptures on pieces of paper and place them where you'll see them often. I have used the bathroom mirror, my car dashboard, and my computer. I simply read some of these scriptures so often that they become second nature, like learning the words of a song. I heard of a man who wrote out every scripture he memorized and put it in a Rolodex that he stored in his car. Every morning he would flip randomly to one card, repeat the scripture, and reflect on it throughout the day. That way he was able to refresh and remember the scriptures he had previously memorized. If you're more of an oral listener, record passages on your smart phone or purchase the Bible on CD or download it to your computer or mobile device.

Second, understand that God has a purpose for your life, and right now His purpose includes loneliness. The feelings you are experiencing are not for lack of reason—God has a purpose in everything He allows us to go through. Romans 8:28 says, "And we know that God causes all things to work together for good to those who love God, to those who are called according to His purpose."

What is it that God is using loneliness to do in your life? Seek out God's design by praying and reading His word. He will reveal to you what lessons you are supposed to learn. Oftentimes it is a sin in our lives that God is seeking to expose. One of the sins He showed me through my loneliness during the early single years was pride. For many years I struggled with this self-consuming sin and wasn't aware of it until I was so adamantly rejected. After the death of my husband, I discovered my severe need for control. Every day I had to trust God to take care of the needs of my children and myself. That was the most challenging walk of faith I've ever been through. But because I was faced with such insurmountable struggles, I appreciated the greatness and faithfulness of God all the more.

The Lord may be using this pain in your life to give you compassion for others. You may consider asking God to show you the people you are being called to serve and help. Begin praying now, and later in the book we will go more in depth as to how to serve others through your suffering.

Whatever the case, if you are looking for the lessons through the difficulties, God will reveal them. You will start to see a theme in conversations and verses that you read. Preachers and teachers may hit on a subject that has particularly stood out to you recently. As you keep your spiritual eyes open for these threads of God's lessons, the Holy Spirit will give you the understanding of what He wants you to learn.

When you are in the face of loneliness, it is easy to let the storms around you distract from what God is accomplishing, but keep your eyes on Christ, and you will see great things. In Matthew 14:28-33, Jesus was walking on the water toward the disciples' boat when He called Peter to come to Him. Peter got out of the boat and walked on the water, "but seeing the wind, he became frightened, and beginning to sink, he cried out, 'Lord, save me!'" (v. 30) Jesus pulled Peter out of the water and said to him, "You of little faith, why did you doubt?" (v. 31).

Peter listened to the call of Christ and believed that he could walk on water. Because of his faith, he performed a great miracle, but when he looked at the circumstances surrounding him, he began to doubt the power of Christ and began to sink. Beware of the storms that come to you during singleness like jealousy, isolation, and bitterness. Keep your eyes on Christ through prayer and strengthening your faith.

Third, if you are dating someone just to keep from being lonely, let it go. Chad had been dating Laura for several months, but he didn't love her. They broke up and got back together many times during this period. As time passed, Laura finally confronted Chad, asking, "Where are we going in this relationship? Are we going to get married?" He answered, "I'm just not ready for that kind of commitment." But the truth was that each time they broke up, Chad couldn't endure being alone, so he reconciled the relationship with Laura just to have company until he met someone whom he thought he could potentially have a future with.

If you're in a relationship like Chad, it isn't fair to you or to the person you're dating to continue when you know that it will not end in marriage. Dating someone to keep from being lonely hurts you in two ways. First, it robs you of the blessings of loneliness and all that God wants to do in your life, and more importantly, it hurts the person you are using for your own selfish gain.

I was the victim of such a scenario. The boyfriend I so wanted to impress didn't want to date me officially, but we spent as much time together talking and kissing as any dating couple. One night I finally confronted him, asking, "Why won't you let me go? Are you just keeping me on the hook, just in case you don't find another girl that you think is better?" At first, he said, no. Then he took it back and hem-hawed around until he finally said, "Maybe." That was the moment I began to see that I was caught in a trap, and I was finally able to find a way out and move on with my life. If you suspect that you're the victim of such selfishness, you probably are. Find the courage to face your single status and move on. Most people won't admit they are using you. (At least my ex-boyfriend had the honesty to do that.) Just cut your ties and get out of it.

Sadly, however, I've also been tempted to be on the using end. After the death of my first husband, I met several wonderful men before I met Robbie, but none seem to be the right fit. I admired qualities of these individuals, and I often tried to talk myself into overlooking the quirks that bothered me. As a result, I felt I inadvertently kept them on a hook of my own as I tried to evaluate whether or not I could make allowances for these issues. It's a delicate balance navigating the emotional boundaries of single friendships and dating.

If you're holding on to a relationship to avoid loneliness, more than likely, fear of being alone is what's causing you to continue, but fear is the opposite of faith. Faith is *trusting* God, while fear is *distrusting*. Remember, you *can* trust Jesus. He made the heavens and the earth, and everything in them. He knows the past, present, and future, and He is the very definition of love (1 John 4:8). It's time to let go of the relationship that may be taking the place of a deeper intimacy with Christ.

Go ahead and walk the invisible bridge of loneliness. Christ will sustain you, and as soon as you place your trust in Him, His presence will comfort you. Proverbs 3:5-6 promises, "Trust in the Lord with all your heart and do not lean on our own understanding. In all your ways acknowledge Him, and He will make your paths straight." Loneliness is the road less traveled, but the end result is a far greater reward.

The Rewards of Faithfulness

As a single, having faith is not as much about taking a vow of celibacy as it is about wanting so desperately to seek after *God's* will for your life that you are willing to do anything, including sacrifice marriage, despite how lonely you might be. I believe in marriage. I've been married twice now, and I've loved both relationships. So I'm not discouraging people from the greatest God-ordained relationship on earth. But for some, that willingness to sacrifice is just what you need to be content as a single person, and for others, that willingness is just where you needed to be in order to find the mate that God has for you.

Before marriage, I struggled a long time with loneliness and had finally come to the conclusion that I was ready to remain single so that I might devote my life entirely to God's work. I had great plans of what I was going to do in the future for Him and for the kingdom. I was already delving into many ministry opportunities that would suffer if I were to have a family, so I was quite satisfied with my single life. I felt honored to sacrifice my dreams of marriage for God's will, and I surrendered my life to His call.

When I met David Beasley, I wasn't thinking marriage at all. As a matter of fact, when he asked me on a date, I went with him only to have something fun to do. I knew that in a few weeks, the opportunity would come to give him my speech about how we weren't right for each other and how I desired to devote my life to ministry.

But the more I got to know David, the more I realized that he was everything I had ever wanted in a husband. We had the strangest things in common—the same quirky sense of humor, the same ideas about family, future, and lifestyle; he even liked to ballroom dance like I do. I have to admit—I was stunned as to why God would call me to be single and yet bring such a wonderful match into my life.

After spending a few weeks with David, I sat down one Sunday afternoon and wrestled with God. I was confused, having been called to singleness and yet meeting a man who was so perfect for me. Was it a test? Was it a distraction? Or was this really the man that I was supposed to marry? As I prayed, the Holy Spirit prompted me to review some of the journal entries that I had written in the past, and I found places where God called me to be faithful, to lay down my pride, and to give up the plans I had for myself, including marriage.

I also found entries where I laid out the desires of my heart, including a list of qualities I wanted in a husband. I wrote:

> *I just got finished attending the third out of 20 weddings I have been invited to this summer, and of course it makes me think about love and marriage.*
>
> *One day, if the timing is right and if you are willing, Lord, I want to be married. We will still be young but old enough to have some wisdom .... When we meet, it won't be love at first sight, but we will have kindred spirits. After bumping into each other everywhere, he'll ask me on a date.*
>
> *... He will love you with all of his heart. He will be a leader with the highest integrity. And he will have never been married. He can sing, but music isn't his passion. He likes to fish and build things. He loves the outdoors, but he wants to live in the city. He laughs a lot, too, and he's very free-spirited.*
>
> *Oh, Father, does this man exist? Should I wait for him? I'm trusting that what they all say is true—that you will let me know when it's the one. I will know. No doubts.*

Reading that was like experiencing the fulfillment of a vision. Those entries described the beginning of our relationship and David's character. I realized then that God wasn't calling me to be single, but He was calling me to be faithful.

I thought of the story of Abraham and Isaac. God had promised Abraham an heir, but his wife, Sarah, was barren. When Abraham was 100 years old, the Lord performed a miracle and finally fulfilled His promise, giving them Isaac.

But in Genesis 22, the Lord called Abraham to sacrifice Isaac. So Abraham took his son, his most precious possession, to the mountain and bound him to the altar. Abraham then took a knife and stretched out his hand to slay his son, when the angel of the Lord stopped him: "By Myself I have sworn, declares the Lord, because you have done this thing and have not withheld your son, your only son, indeed I will greatly bless you … In your seed all the nations of the earth shall be blessed, because you have obeyed My voice" (vv. 16-18).

Just as God called Abraham to sacrifice Isaac, God called me to give up my desire to be married, not because He wanted me to be single at the time, but because He wanted me to be *faithful*.

By the end of that Sunday, I knew that this relationship was from God. In my journal I wrote, "Lord, I feel like I could give a life-long commitment to this man. I feel like this relationship is from you, but if you would rather I remain single, I would do anything for you. If you ask me to sacrifice him, I will."

Three months later, we were engaged, and I knew David was the one. No doubts.

When David died, I had to come to terms with the fact that the gift that God gave to me was His to take away, as the servant Job exclaimed, "The Lord giveth and the Lord taketh away. Blessed be the name of the Lord." What I wrote in my journal all those many years ago, I meant. "If you ask me to sacrifice him, I will."

It was a brutal sacrifice, but I don't despise it. I can see the purposes in all of it, and the many ways God prepared me for its coming. I don't have the space to explain all the ways He equipped me for the moment my life would change forever, but it was clear to me that I was not forgotten. All the study I did for this book alone (mostly completed during our married years) was just the foundation for the real test of suffering and loneliness to come. The thought that my experience may bring someone to Christ or draw a brother or sister closer to our Lord is what gives me the greatest pleasure and hope. That's what makes the sacrifice worth it.

I was widowed three years when I met Robbie McDonald. He was a widower himself, and I felt an immediate connection with him because of our shared experiences. As a Christian, I saw the characteristics of a man that I knew would take care of me and my children, the way he cared so tenderly for his ailing wife. I studied the character of his two sons and listened to his testimony. I considered whether or not we could minister together in the church and how we complimented each other.

Most of all, I prayed about whether or not this is what God wanted. As difficult as it was to be a single mom, I was more than willing to face the loneliness if that was the calling of God. In the end, I believe God showed me that the children needed a father in their lives to be that example of our heavenly Father, and Robbie was the kind of man that I could love, be proud of, and serve faithfully.

What about you? Is God calling you to give up your plans and accept His? Are you willing to lay down your Isaac? Seek your heart, and ask God to show you the areas in your life where you need to let go of control. Then be willing to accept it. When you do, you will experience the blessings of sacrifice as the peace of God guides your heart and shows you the answers that you have been seeking.

Chapter 6

The Blessings of Service

"The harvest is plentiful but the workers are few."
-Matthew 9:37-38

I was having dinner at a conference, sitting at a table with several different women I had just met. Next to me sat a couple of ladies, both in their early to mid thirties, and neither had ever been married. The first told her friend, "I am so tired of being a built-in babysitter. It seems like my married friends only call me when they want me to watch their kids, but I have a life, too. Just because I'm not married doesn't mean I'm always available."

Her friend was sympathetic, yet she didn't find herself with the same sentiments. The woman explained to her friend that she babysat quite often for some married friends, but didn't feel used at all. As a matter of fact, she felt that it was an excellent opportunity to spend time with the kids because they saw her as an aunt. She honestly considered this couple to be a brother and sister.

Both of these women were often called to serve their married friends, but one found only bitterness and resentment, and the other found a family. The second of these two women saw her singleness from a completely different perspective—a godly perspective. She had the heart of a servant.

A servant is someone who spends her time focusing on the needs of other people, sharing her physical and spiritual resources with an attitude of generosity. Servants put the needs of others before themselves and usually do the jobs that most people wouldn't do. To sustain this kind of lifestyle takes a humble heart, one like Christ. Jesus said that He came to this earth not to *be* served but *to serve* (Matthew 20:28).

I once heard someone say the only thing you can take with you to heaven is other people. What an eye-opener! Money, goods, and even marital status will have no use in heaven. Riches and position will have no value, so to put stock in treasures like these is useless. People, on the other hand, last for eternity, whether they are in heaven or hell. Jesus tells us in Matthew 6:19-22, "Do not store up for yourselves treasure on earth, where moth and rust destroy, and where thieves break in and steal, but store up for yourselves treasures in heaven, where neither moth nor rust destroys, and where thieves do not break in or steal; for where your treasure is, there your heart will be also." If you want to capitalize on something, think of the long term … the very long term. People are the only guaranteed investment that will last for eternity.

Imagine if you were given two choices to grow your money—one was guaranteed to make you rich in two years and then crash, leaving you in poverty, and the other was a slower increase, but would leave you a millionaire when you retire—which would you choose? If you were wise, you would choose the long-term goal. It's the same when we choose where to invest our lives. We could choose to spend our time indulging in our own pleasures, which only lasts a short while, or we could put our time and resources into something of far greater value—the lives of others.

Some singles may hear me say, "Invest in people," and respond, "What better way to accomplish this than by marrying one!" But not even marriage will last for eternity. There is no marriage in heaven (Mark 12:24-25), so if your life revolves around finding a mate, you are running after things that are temporal. I'm not saying that marriage is wrong or not appropriate for believers—that particular relationship has great value for this life, not the least of which is the reason we discussed earlier: marriage is a reflection of God's love for His people. But it is only a reflection. When this earth passes away, there will be no more need for marriage between a man and a woman—we will be united with the Bridegroom Christ.

To invest in people means to take the time, energy, and money you would normally put into something earthly, like a career, possessions, or experiences, and learn to put those commodities toward building into the lives of people around you. When you do that, the gospel is shared, God is glorified, and others may come to know Christ either for the first time or know Him in a deeper way as a result.

What it Means to be a Servant

I once heard an acquaintance of mine say, "I am so tired of hearing how singles can serve other people because they supposedly have so much 'extra time.' I don't have extra time for anything!" I understand her frustration—in such a fast-paced world, no one feels like they have "extra time." But she was wrong in her attitude that she shouldn't be expected to serve. We are *all* called to serve, no matter how much time we have—married and single alike.

When Christ was on this earth, He thought of Himself as a servant of men (Philippians 2:7). As a matter of fact, although He was God, He was made a little lower than the angels (Hebrews 2:7). He washed feet, healed the sick, taught the word of God, and fed the multitudes. His entire life from beginning to end was lived to pour into the people around Him. We, too, are called to be like Christ in this way, and loneliness can be the tool to drive it into our lives.

When I first realized that my loneliness could be a tool to help me minister to others, my perspective changed, and therefore, my life transformed. I started using my flexible schedule to focus on grow spiritually. I read Christian growth books by some of the world's most renowned theologians. I started a women's Bible study that met at my house each week, which continued for two years, reaching approximately 30-45 single women within the church. I served on the worship team, and I had a personal ministry of meeting new girls to make them feel welcome.

After having been married and now raising two small children, I can honestly say that I would never have time to do all of these things as a wife or a young mother. That's not to say that I won't be able to have a ministry at all, but while my children are still at this early state, my attention is divided. I now have a family to care for, and that is a job that continues 24 hours a day and seven days a week. No weekends. No holidays. Since parenting is such a great ministry in itself, it's not easy to find time for a multitude of activities. I'm grateful that God gave me the grace to take advantage of my pre-married single years when I had them.

My friend Bobbie also found joy in using her singleness to serve others. She had just moved into a new apartment and was applying for a job when she realized that she wasn't listening to God's call to embrace her loneliness. She says:

> *I thought I was doing the right thing, but God kept pleading on my heart to use my time wisely ... embrace the gift of singleness. I kept thinking about this over and over and finally one day after two weeks of being in my apartment, I decided to quit my new job, move to a residential camp to work with youth. I even had to get rid of my dog, but that was so good for me. God used that moment in my life to lift me up and show me where I was still harboring my deepest pain. In giving of my singleness, embracing my loneliness, and having a broken spirit, God shown brightly in my life during that time. That year is one of the deepest parts embedded in my soul.*
>
> *I had times in my life where I partied and danced and had a million so called friends, but nothing compares to the memory of seeing God shining in the eyes of those children and in the eyes of those who work there.*

It is the love of God within us that drives us to serve not only Him but also our brothers and sisters in Christ. To see ourselves as servants takes us from any lofty position in our minds to a lowly place, where we say, "I deserve nothing; it is a privilege just to serve the kingdom." After reaching that place of humility, it's so easy to find joy! That change in perspective shows the magnificence of God's grace, as we see our place in the kingdom in comparison of who God is.

Jesus said, "The harvest is plentiful but the workers are few" (Matthew 9:37-38). If you want to reap a harvest of joy and purpose, then volunteer to work in the fields. As singles, you have expendable time and flexible schedules. That is not to say that your time can't get filled up, but the hours are more accommodating. Most married people don't have the blessing of expendable time tables, particularly when they have children. The dinner must be cooked, the house cleaned, the dishes washed, the bed made, the dog let out, the babies put to bed, and there must be time left for intimacy and communication between a husband and wife.

It's true that singles have chores to do, as well, but as one single friend said, "It doesn't matter that my clothes are on the floor in my room and I grab something quick to eat—my schedule is my own, so if I want to spend more time away from my home, I can."

If you don't think you have a lot of extra time, let me challenge you to turn off your television for a month. Don't even watch the news—listen to it on the radio or read the paper if you want, but take the television out of your life for four weeks. You may find that you have more time than you think you do.

This isn't a comparison of how much free time married people have versus singles; we are all busy, and each of us is given 24 hours in a day, no more. But I want to challenge singles to see the time that they spend "being lonely" as a gift. Don't waste it on mindless television programs or stewing in self-pity.

I remember when a dear friend called me one day. We have known each other since college, and both of us have a heart for ministry. At the time, she was married, and I was single. We hadn't talked in a few months, so she called just to catch up and see what was new in my life. I told her about the things God was doing through me—Bible studies, ministering to women, singing on the worship team. I told her about the growth I was seeing in the girls that were coming to the study and the great things God was teaching me.

My friend had just recently had her second child and was discovering how difficult it is to be responsible for not just one life but two. She then confessed to me that she envied the fact that I was involved in so many ministries. It wasn't an angry envy but one that partly wished she was single again and able to be so involved, even though it meant dealing with loneliness.

As a mother myself, I understand parenting is a place of ultimate servanthood, but my friend saw what God was doing in my life to make a difference in so many others. 1 Corinthians 7:32-34 tells us that a wife and mother are concerned about her husband and children, but a single woman has the ability to be concerned only about the things of God. The Apostle Paul writes:

> *But I want you to be free from concern. One who is unmarried is concerned about the things of the Lord, how he may please the Lord; but one who is married, is concerned about the things of the world, how he may please his wife, and his interests are divided. The woman who is unmarried, and the virgin, is concerned about*

the things of the Lord, that she may be holy both in body and spirit; but one who is married is concerned about the things of the world, how she may please her husband.

Being a mother or father is often glorified by singles, but even before I was ever a biological mother, I was a *spiritual* mother, teaching others, leading others, and in some cases, introducing others to the love of Christ by investing in the lives of the people around me and seeing myself as a servant of the Lord.

Paul said in 1 Corinthians 9:19, "For though I am free from all men, I have made myself a slave to all, so that I may win more." The glorious part of being a servant is the ability to point others to Christ. No matter if we are married or single, all of us are called to reach others with the Good News. To serve is the greatest fulfillment for anyone who calls himself a follower of Christ. Just as Paul said in 2 Corinthians 4:5, "For we do not preach ourselves but Christ Jesus as Lord, and ourselves as your bond-servants for Jesus' sake."

The Right Reasons

I must mention that there is a heart of service that is not a blessing but a burden, and that is when your service is done out of a desire to impress others or validate your worth. Service should be done from a heart to glorify only one person—God. When you choose to serve others for your own personal glory, you will fail every time, sinking into more misery, unable to experience the blessings of service. In Matthew 6:1, Jesus said, "Beware of practicing your righteousness before men to be noticed by them; otherwise you have no reward with your Father who is in heaven." When you serve, do it from a heart that desires for God to get the glory, not yourself.

In the same way, service should not be used to snag a date. I have known many single women who attempt to be service-oriented in front of men in order to appear more domestic. These women theorize that if they do many acts of service, like cook meals, show hospitality, or host events, then single men will be more attracted to them. Not only does this serve a selfish purpose, it is also deceptive. You may convince a man that you are more "domesticated" than most women, but unless you are able to live up to that standard after marriage, then you have both hurt yourself and the man you deceived.

Service can also be used to isolate you from others rather then build into others. I used to be a part of a guest care team for the singles event at church. We had dinners once a month to which we invited new attendees. All of us on the team pitched in to help, but there was one girl in particular who was a very hard worker. She made sure the food was prepared just right, the bread warmed in the oven. She walked around the room and picked up the plates and trash that were left over. Then when everyone was basically finished with the meal, she started putting away all of the dishes and packing up the food. By the time she was finished, the last of the guests were walking out the door.

One night I notice her hard labor. I thought, *She is working so hard. Isn't anyone helping her? I wonder what I could do to help, but then I would have to leave the girls that I came here to talk to. Isn't that the reason why I'm here? Not to work on the presentation of the food or the house but to minister to these women?*

Then I realized, she wasn't working because all of these things needed to be done right away. She was working because she wanted to find a way to hide from people. Service gave her the excuse not to engage in a relationship with anyone. By keeping busy, she had the excuse of "no time" to keep her from facing her fear of others.

Jesus rebuked Martha of the same sin in Luke 10:38-42. Mary sat at Jesus' feet, spending her time with Him and listening to His teaching, and Martha labored with meal preparations. Then Martha became angry with Mary for leaving her with all the work. But Jesus said, "Martha, Martha, you are worried and bothered about so many things; but only one thing is necessary, for Mary has chosen the good part, which shall not be taken away from her."

There is time for working in the kitchen and preparing, but there is also time for doing things of the Lord. When we spend time ministering to others, we are engaging in fellowship with Jesus. Matthew 25:44-45 says, "Then they themselves also will answer, 'Lord, when did we see You hungry, or thirsty, or a stranger, or naked, or sick, or in prison, and did not take care of You?' Then He will answer them, 'Truly I say to you, to the extent that you did not do it to one of the least of these, you did not do it to Me.'"

70

The Image of a Bond-Servant

I met Margie Rich, an 88-year-old woman who understood what it meant to invest in the lives of people. When her husband died 25 years previously, Margie used her experience of going through the death of a spouse to minister to other widows. She started a thriving ministry at Quaker Gardens Retirement and Health Facility in Stanton, Calif., where she was living. "I just live my life for Christ," Margie said. "My apartment is my chapel and without having to cook and clean, I have the time to pray and prepare lessons for the people I minister to."

Instead of mourning her loneliness and wallowing in self-pity, Margie used her time as a widow to the kingdom's fullest advantage. For example, engaged couples and newlyweds who knew Margie through Quaker Gardens staff and her home church came to her for pre-marital counseling. She offered them advice, books, and resources.

But that's only part of a ministry schedule so full that Margie used a personal day calendar to keep up with her routine. Once a week, she visited the facility's nursing home. Margie also took time each week to read the Bible to a sister in Christ who had lost her eyesight. While there, she welcomed the other residents to gather around and listen.

Margie facilitated a number of Bible studies for residents and staff members alike. At one point, she was meeting with four pupils a week to discuss Bible lessons one-to-one.

Some of her other activities included speaking at devotionals, pushing residents who are in wheelchairs to chapel for worship, encouraging the more than 1,000 visitors she had received since she moved into Quaker Gardens, and keeping in touch with people through e-mail.

Once a month, Margie visited those with severe ailments like Alzheimer's and dementia, all the time praying for those to whom she felt spiritually drawn. "One man in here said that, when he lost his wife, he lost his life," Margie said. "I told him that when I lost my husband I just went on with my life [in Christ]."

Margie Rich understood what it means to use her singleness to the fullness of Christ. Yes, she loved her husband deeply, but when he died her life moved on in her love of Jesus. When other widows were falling apart in their pain, Margie was teaching them how to find contentment in her Lord.

Learning to be a Servant

Being a servant is not so much about using all of your time focusing on works, but it's more in the attitude of the heart. In order to renew your mind to be a servant, meditate on servanthood, practice it, and the more you do that, the easier it will become. Consider these points as you seek to bless others through service.

First, a servant seeks humility, not praise. When serving, don't expect appreciation or a pat on the back, but work because you are by nature a servant of God, seeking His glory, not your own. I once heard of a man named Joe who was the janitor of a large church and private Christian school. When Joe met the students in the hall he always stopped one of them and asked, "Are you excited about Jesus today?" Then he would proceed to ask what God was doing in that student's life and share what God was doing in his own.

One Sunday, Joe was asked to give his testimony to the church. "It doesn't matter what you do as long as you do it for God's glory," he said. "[Even though I'm just a janitor] I feel as fulfilled as any business owner. God is pleased with me." Joe didn't strive for earthly rewards, but he sought to invest in the lives of the students, even as the janitor. He understood what Paul meant by being content in all circumstances (Philippians 4:11) and to do all things to the glory of God.

The next time you are asked to participate in some type of service, check your attitude. Did you receive the opportunity with joy or reluctance? Would God appreciate your humility or are you guilty of thinking that you are too important to serve in that capacity? If you find that your outlook needs adjusting, pray and ask God to give you the heart of a servant.

Get started now. Perform a kind act of service today without receiving any praise. Send an anonymous word of encouragement or a financial gift. Volunteer for a job that usually goes unnoticed, and don't share the experience with anyone, even a friend or family member. Let it be a secret joy between you and God. In Matthew 6:1-4, Jesus explains the value of indiscretion:

Beware of practicing your righteousness before men to be noticed by them; otherwise you have no reward with your Father who is in heaven. So when you give to the poor, do not sound a trumpet before you, as the hypocrites do in the synagogues and in the streets, so that they may be honored by men. Truly I say to you, they have their reward in full. But when you give to the poor, do not let your left hand know what your right hand is doing, so that your giving will be in secret; and your Father who sees what is done in secret will reward you.

I don't know about you, but I would rather have a reward that comes from God than from men! I will admit it feels good to be admired and praised by your peers, but by avoiding the temptation of temporal acclaim, we are investing in eternal returns.

Second, a servant obeys the master. We must learn to obey the commands of the Lord, even when He asks us to serve in the most undesirable ways. At my house there are some jobs that no one wants to do—clean the toilets, empty the trash, and wash the dog—but someone must be willing to do it. Just think what the house would be like if these chores went unfinished.

As a single, maybe God is calling you to do a job that you don't want to do, like volunteer at a nursing home or church nursery. Maybe He is calling you to be single for a long time, so that you may better serve Him. Maybe He is calling you to give more of your disposable income to the service of Christ. Mother Teresa once said, "Let us not love in words but let us love until it hurts. It hurt Jesus to love us: He died for us. And today it is your turn and my turn to love one another as Jesus loved us."[7] Christ isn't asking us to do anything that He hasn't done already for us. To serve others is to return what we ourselves have already received.

Make a commitment to the Lord that you will serve Him in any capacity, no matter how unpleasant the job may seem. Ask Him what He would have you do and then do it. Here are some ways that you can serve:

- Set up a time to baby-sit for married friends. Many parents need one-on-one time to build their relationship, and the only way they get that time is when someone is willing to watch their kids. The parents will come home renewed and grateful for your services.

- Set aside some time to visit the elderly. Many elderly people are very lonely and don't often get visitors. Time spent with younger people make them feel loved and appreciated. A visit like this

73

isn't just beneficial to them; you will be enriched with the wisdom of their lives, as well.

- Sometimes weddings are not fun for singles, especially if you long for nuptials of your own one day. Although it can be hard, weddings are the perfect opportunities to selflessly serve. Volunteer to serve the bride's family by taking candid photos, passing out birdseed, running last-minute errands, or baby-sitting for mothers who are in the wedding. In this case, being alone can be a great asset as you selflessly help someone else enjoy his or her wedding day to the fullest.

- No one understands loneliness more deeply than an orphan. You may consider starting an orphans ministry in your church.

Third, a servant is grateful. Growing up, my family was very poor, so what others might have taken for granted, we appreciated. One time we couldn't afford bath tissue, so for Christmas, my mother asked her family to include some in the Christmas packages they sent. That's a commodity that most people take for granted. When you have it, you hardly notice, but when you don't have it, it's quite obvious!

In the same way, singleness can be taken for granted. There is a lot of freedom and flexibility available to you. Have you thanked God for the gift He has given you? It's easy to be bitter when you feel lonely. Ask the Lord to turn your bitterness into thanksgiving and then look for the good in your situation. Philippians 2:14-15 says, "Do all things without grumbling or disputing; so that you will prove yourselves to be blameless and innocent, children of God above reproach in the midst of a crooked and perverse generation, among whom you appear as lights in the world..."

If you're having a hard time coming up with reasons to be thankful, start a list. Write down as many positive aspects about singleness that you can think of and then write out a prayer to God telling Him how grateful you are for your circumstances. Keep the list handy for times when you need some encouragement.

As you seek to serve the Lord, you will find a deep sense of personal fulfillment. You will be able to look back at all the ways you touched lives and brought about tangible gifts to those around you. The book of

James reminds us how important our works of service are to our professed faith. "What good is it, my brothers and sisters, if someone claims to have faith but does not have works? Can this kind of faith save him? If a brother or sister is poorly clothed and lacks daily food, and one of you says to them, 'Go in peace, keep warm and eat well,' but you do not give them what the body needs, what good is it?" (2:14-16). Acts of service give substance to the life we claim to live in Christ.

As a result of your good works, you will come away with gifts of gratefulness, humility, and peace, among others. There is hardly a better reward on this earth than the feeling of a contented heart that is bursting forth with joy when you retire in your bed at night. This is just another one of the great blessings that can characterize the life of a single person who takes advantage of the blessings of loneliness.

Chapter 7

The Blessings of Waiting

"I stand at the door and knock"
-Revelations 3:20

When I was a little girl, my best friend, Kathleen, and I loved to play with Barbie® dolls. One of our favorite activities was creating Barbie weddings. In one of the most memorable weddings, Kathleen brought to my house every Barbie and Ken doll she could find. Together we had over 100 dolls—it was an entire village! We dressed one in a wedding gown and her beau in his tux. And the oldest of the Kens played the part of the pastor.

During the wedding, the Barbies sat in rows as they watched the bride and groom walk down a tissue aisle to unite their plastic lives. They exchanged vows, and we cut out a small piece of paper and wrote out a tiny marriage license with dates and their full names. At the end of the ceremony, we took pictures of the happy couple and snapped a photo of the bride throwing her bouquet.

Little girls always dream about weddings. Even as young as we were, our dreams revolved around our own future wedding days. As long as I can remember, I've had a vision for the day I would become a bride—red roses for my bouquet, romantic music, ballroom dancing, and classic vows. But despite all of my youthful planning, when I was old enough to get married—still longing for dreams of blissful love—I was missing something … a groom.

My single life started out as a quest to find my lost groom. I tried dozens of relationships all based on romance and emotions, but they were futile. By my senior year of college, most of my friends were engaged, and I felt left out. Over the summer I started dating a guy, and I remember telling my roommate, "This is the man I'm going to marry. I know that because I *have* to marry him—he's my last chance."

Our relationship became problematic after only a few weeks of dating, but I was willing to marry him because I thought marriage would make my life complete. Then I would be happy like everyone else, I reasoned.

Something made me feel less than adequate if I didn't keep up with my friends in the relationship realm. The comparison made me unhappy with the place God had me as a single. Fear drove me to make bad decisions—I didn't want to be left out of something that everyone else had. I thought by not having a boyfriend or fiancé, I appeared to be unwanted. Instead of putting my faith in Christ and trusting that He had a sovereign plan for me, I put my trust in romance to bring purpose to my life and define who I was.

There was a woman in the Bible who also tried to find fulfillment through earthly relationships, but her life was changed the day she met Jesus at Jacob's well in Samaria. When she came to the well, she was not only thirsty from the dryness of the desert, but also within her soul.

We learn through the dialogue of their conversation that this woman had been married five times and she was currently living with a man who was not her husband. She was obviously trying to quench her thirst through relationships, but they never satisfied. "Everyone who drinks of this water shall thirst again," Jesus told the woman, "but whoever drinks of the water that I will give him shall never thirst; but the water that I will give him will become in him a well of water springing up to eternal life" (John 4:13-14).

That day, Jesus gave this woman water that reached her heart and she was finally filled—she had been given new life. As a result, she testified to those in her village, and they believed in Jesus, as well.

Like this woman, I also came to a place where I finally understood that Christ meant more to me than any relationship of this world. I realized that I didn't need an earthly groom to fulfill me; I already had a relationship with the One who loved me more than anyone could ever love me.

By His grace, God was merciful and kept me from marrying that boyfriend. For months I tried to keep the relationship alive. There were misunderstandings, bitterness, verbal abuse, and paranoia on both sides of the relationship that resulted in a lot of scarring and tearing. And all the time, Christ kept wooing me back to himself, back to the One who loved me, to the One who understood the rejection I felt deep within my heart. The more pain I experienced within the relationship, the more I wanted only to be with Jesus, where I felt safe and secure.

Everything in life felt like it was crashing down around me, but the Cornerstone was still there to give me the foundation that I needed. On January 6, 2001, after months of pain, feeling lonely and rejected, I understood the basic beauty of living in Christ. I wrote in my journal:

> *Jesus, you are my friend; you saved me from hell and when I die, I will go to Heaven. You have saved me from a meaningless life. You are pleasant to be around; You are like a cool breeze each time you speak to me, and I don't know how the world can live without you ... I am so thankful to have known you, and even if you never bless me again as long as I live, just knowing you is enough to sustain me.*

Are you satisfied with Him alone? Have you, like the woman at the well, tried to satisfy your thirst through the endless pursuit of relationships? When was the last time you tasted the life-giving water of Christ? He is ready and available for you to come to Him at any time. Everyone is welcome to drink of His life-giving water.

The True Bridegroom

Jesus refers to Himself as "the bridegroom" in the gospels of the New Testament (Matthew 9:15, Matthew 25:1-10, Mark 2:19-20, Luke 5:34-35). In John 3:29, John the Baptist refers to himself as the best man, who comes before the groom. As an unmarried woman, the whole time I was looking for a groom to fulfill me, I didn't realize I already had one with whom I would be united for *eternity*, not just during this life on earth.

Stop and imagine yourself for a moment waiting for the bridegroom to receive you. His best man announces His coming, and when the door opens, the man standing in front of you is the King of kings and the Lord of lords, waiting for you with open arms. This man who is the embodiment of perfection has chosen *you* to spend the rest of eternity with Him! Isaiah 62:5 says, "As a bridegroom rejoices over his bride, so will your God rejoice over you."

You may be lonely on this earth, but you have hope of eternity. We have a Bridegroom, but we must wait patiently for Him to come back and take us to His home. As you wait on Christ to receive you, learn to devote yourself completely to Him.

One day all of us will be united with our Groom, so every relationship on earth should come second to that one. Remember that marriage was given to us so that it would reflect Christ's love for His church (Ephesians 5). Too many singles are busy making mate-hunting a priority that their relationship with Christ suffers. Yet, that is the very relationship that will last throughout eternity, unlike any other.

Even a good marriage won't sustain you. You need Christ. Both of my marriages were wonderful. I have loved both of these men deeply, but neither were ever perfect. You can't depend on marriage to fulfill you because it can (and will eventually) end. Some marriages end in divorce, or like mine, they can end in tragedy. But all of them will end one day in the death of one or the other mate. Better to put your hope in Christ who will never leave you or forsake you.

Several weeks before my first husband died I began to wonder if I had put too much of my attention and affection on David, making him some kind of idol in my life. I believe these thoughts were God's way of preparing me for the overwhelming loss and reminding me that God was my sustainer, not David.

For three years I was a single girl working at FamilyLife, a marriage and family subsidiary of Campus Crusade for Christ. Since I was involved in promotion of their marriage conferences, I attended many of them. The conference that I worked with focused primarily on the wedding vows, and at the end of each event, all of the couples held hands, looked into each other's eyes and renewed their matrimonial promises to each other.

The first time I attended one of these events, I wasn't sure what to do. Here I was a single girl sitting in the audience while everyone else stood with their spouses. I got out of my chair with the other couples, but I had no mate to gaze at. For a moment I felt awkward standing there alone. Then I remembered that I am never alone, but Christ is with me—my

Bridegroom. In the middle of all of these couples, I looked up to heaven and repeated each of the marriage vows to my Bridegroom, listening with my heart to His promises to me.

It was a beautiful moment that still lives in my mind. It defined my dedication to Christ, just as a wedding is the moment that marks your dedication to a spouse. In my joy of committing to Christ as His bride, I was later inspired to rewrite Psalm 23 in my own words as an ode to my Lord, my Husband:

"The Lord Is My Husband"

The Lord is my Husband,
in heart we are one.
He comforts me in my loneliness;
He brings me peace in times of trouble;
He makes me whole.
He always tells me He loves me for my hope's sake.
Yea, though my life is filled with physical loneliness,
I am never alone; for He is with me.
His touch and His smile they comfort me.
He prepares me for the future by teaching me submission through pain;
He forgives my sin with acceptance;
His grace runneth over.
Surely fulfillment and contentment will be a part of my life,
and the favor of God will shine in my heart forever.

What steps have you taken to refresh your devotion to your Lord? Have you ever considered yourself as His bride? Do you anticipate His return? Here are a few suggestions on how to remind yourself that you are the bride of Christ:

First, *make a list of Christ's promises to you.* Research the scriptures through Bible dictionaries and concordances. (There's one in the back of most Bibles.) Write down the reference and a note to explain each time you read a scripture that contains a promise from Christ to His people. You will find most of the words of Christ in first our books of the New Testament.

As you read through your list, write down the ways in which the Lord has fulfilled those promises in your life. Then give Him thanks for all that

He has done. Be specific in your descriptions and spend time meditating on each one.

Here are some examples of the promises you may find:

- "I am with you always, even to the end of the age" (Matthew 28:20).
- "If you continue in My word, then you are truly disciples of Mine; and you will know the truth, and the truth will make you free" (John 8:32).
- "The thief comes only to steal and kill and destroy; I came that they may have life, and have it abundantly" (John 10:10).

Second, *find some symbol of His affection for you and place it where you can see it often.* In the Old Testament, the children of Israel used "stones of remembrance" to mark places where God spoke to them so that they might remember His instructions or His miracles (see Exodus 28:12, Joshua 4:5-7). In the same way, the symbol you choose should remind you of Christ's love and dedication to you.

A Catholic friend once told me that nuns wear wedding bands as a reminder of their marriage to Christ. They even change their name, just like a bride would do. What beautiful imagery! After my friend shared this with me, I was so moved by the power of the symbolism, that for a time, I wore a band made out of hematite, a black stone, on my right ring finger. The band reminded me of Christ's everlasting devotion to me, and the black color symbolized my own death.

I'm not suggesting that you convert to Catholicism or even start wearing rings, but I am suggesting that you choose something to remind you that you are the property of Christ. I used a ring to symbolize His love. Perhaps you could wear a special necklace or bracelet. Or place a painting or other artwork in your workspace, so that you are reminded of His love each day as you work.

Take time to pick out something that is symbolic in color, style, and substance. You may choose something that is made of a specific substance, like gold to remind you of God's pure, unconditional love. You may choose something of a significant color, like a blue stone to remind you of His loyalty. Some singles choose to have these objects engraved with an important verse that proclaims God's promises.

Third, be intimate with Him. A marriage could not survive between a man and a woman if they were not intimate with each other. By intimate, I mean that a husband and wife know things about each other that no one else knows. They are completely naked in front of each other and are not ashamed, physically or emotionally, because there are no secrets between them.

Strive to have this kind of closeness with Christ. Be honest with Him. Tell Him the desires of your heart and the gut-wrenching feelings that overwhelm you, including hurts and hopes.

In return, learn all about Him. If you had an earthly fiancé, you would be so madly in love with him that you would crave to know all about his life, character, and thoughts. If he wrote a book for you, wouldn't you relish every word? You wouldn't be able to put it down!

God *has* written a love letter to you, and it's called the Bible. John 1:14 says that Jesus is the Word made flesh, so if you want to know Him intimately, you must know the word of which He is the embodiment. Learn about His life on earth in the Gospels, read and understand His words, study the way He lives His life. The more you understand the heart of Christ, the more your faith will grow. Have you ever taken the time to read it—all of it? If you haven't read the scriptures all the way through, let me challenge you to do it—start in Genesis and go all the way through to Revelation. Instead of picking up a novel, magazine, or turning on the TV, use that time to read the Bible bit by bit. Commit to reading three chapters a day, and you will have the entire book read in approximately one year. Psalms 1:1-3 says:

> *How blessed is the man who does not walk in the counsel of the wicked, nor stand in the path of sinners, nor sit in the seat of scoffers! But his delight is in the law of the Lord, and in His law he meditates day and night. He will be like a tree firmly planted by streams of water, which yields fruit in its season and its leaf does not wither; And in whatever he does he prospers.*

Another way to grow more intimate with Christ is through prayer. 1 Thessalonians 5:17 tells us to "pray without ceasing," which is to say, communicate with Christ continuously. He's with you no matter where you go, so talk to Him in your car while you drive, in the shower, and at night before bed. Prayer means to communicate with God, so it's not necessary that your eyes always be closed and your head bowed. Just talk to Him.

Remember that prayer is a two-way conversation—you're not the only one communicating. You may not hear an audible voice, but when the Spirit speaks, you will have an understanding in your heart and mind. Allow enough silence in your prayer time to hear what He is saying to you. Don't just ramble for the sake of filling the silence. It's okay if there are some still moments.

Fourth, honor Him. As the bride of Christ, you will be given a new name (Revelation 2:17, Isaiah 56:5, Isaiah 62:2, Isaiah 65:15), just as a bride is given a new name. My maiden name was Joyce, and my married name is McDonald. Just by my name everyone knows that I am the wife of a man named McDonald, so whatever I do, it reflects on his family.

It is the same with Christ. We carry the name "Christian" and whatever we do, it reflects on Jesus. We must live in a way that gives Him glory, not cause Him sorrow. Ephesians 4:30 says, "Do not grieve the Holy Spirit of God by whom you were sealed for the day of redemption." As the bride of Christ, take a look at your spiritual garments. Is there anything soiling your gown? Are you fit to receive the Groom? Examine your heart today and if you find anything not fit for the bride of Christ, ask Him to cleanse you and He will be faithful to do so (1 John 1:9).

Another way to honor Christ is to speak of Him boldly and with admiration. My husband is blessed when he hears me tell others about how proud I am of Him. His face lights up because it pleases him that I am pleased.

Let everyone know that you belong to Christ. Any bride-to-be is proud of her fiancé. She shows off her ring of promise and proclaims to everyone the good news of their marriage. When was the last time you spoke of your Groom with admiration? When was the last time you told your friends what He has done for you?

An Eternal Perspective

As I mentioned earlier, marriage doesn't last forever (Mark 12:25). It was created to be a reflection of the relationship between Christ and the Church, so when we are reunited with the Bridegroom, there will be no more need for reflections—we will be living with the reality of it

(Ephesians 5:22-32). Marriage as we know it will no longer exist, so if we make marriage the goal of our lives, then we have wasted the time God has given us for a certain purpose. Marriage is a noble estate for those who are called to it, but even then marriage is only a *part* of the journey, not the end.

I believe the reason why so many singles are unsatisfied with their status is because they have a vague, if existing, view of eternity. The Bible instructs us to set our minds on things of heaven, not on things of earth. Colossians 3:1-4 says:

> *Therefore if you have been raised up with Christ, keep seeking the things above, where Christ is, seated at the right hand of God. Set your mind on the things above, not on the things that are on earth. For you have died and your life is hidden with Christ in God. When Christ, who is our life, is revealed, then you also will be revealed with Him in glory.*

To set marriage as your life's goal is to set your mind on the things of the earth. King David referred to the passing of life as grass that withers away in the sun (Psalm 37:2). In the same way, we are only on earth for a short while and then we will pass into eternity. 1 John 2:17 says, "The world is passing away, and also its lusts; but the one who does the will of God lives forever."

Have you ever sat down to think about just *how long* eternity is? It never ends! Think of a life that never ends. Just image yourself 100 years from now. Now imagine yourself after 1,000 years, a million—then double it, and double that … It goes on and on—it's mind boggling! To think that there will be no more death, but only life everlasting. It makes this life on earth seem so short.

If there is such little time on earth, why do we take the precious amount we have to concentrate on an investment that will not last forever? Instead of pledging your devotion to seek a relationship of this earth, pledge yourself to fulfilling the call of Christ. I'm not insisting that no one get married—that would be ridiculous. Marriage is a beautiful and God-honoring institution. But it should not be the *goal* of life. You can trust God—if marriage is part of your calling, then God will provide a spouse for you.

Don't try to cure your loneliness with marriage, but allow it to draw you closer to Christ. When you do, you will be filled with His pleasure, and the loneliness will not seem like loneliness at all, but rather a gateway from this dying world to a world of abundant life.

This planet is not our home, but as believers our citizenship is in heaven (Philippians 3:20). We are told in Hebrews 11:13-16 that we are "aliens and strangers, waiting for another heavenly place." Heaven is where our dreams should reside, not earth. Is marriage important? Yes, for those who are called to it, because it is a reflection of God's love. But is it necessary for the kingdom and our future home with Christ? No. He is all we need to fulfill our lives now and forever.

Jesus is Alive!

I have heard many singles say, "Yes, I know that God loves me, but I want to be loved by a *real* person." I was in a meeting of newlyweds not long ago and one girl said, "Singleness was good, but marriage is better because you have someone to share life with."

Her statement astounded me. Where is her faith? Is Christ dead? Are we the bride of a ghost who once lived but has passed away? No, He is alive! This young woman already *had* someone to share her life with, but she apparently didn't make the most of that relationship when she was single. For me, my pre-married years were a time when I was most intimate with Christ and if anything, I struggled as a newlywed because I missed my time with the Healer and the Lover of my Soul.

I think we forget that Jesus *is* a real person. He's not just a good person who once lived. He's not just an idea or an inspiration. He is the King of kings and Lord of lords (1 Timothy 6:15-16) who is at this moment at the right hand of God (Hebrews 8:1), interceding for us (Romans 8:34), and one day He is coming back to receive us into heaven (Luke 12:25-40), so we need to be waiting for Him and looking in the clouds (Revelation 1:7)—it could even be *this very day!*

In Matthew 25:1-11 Jesus tells the parable of the 10 virgins, who were waiting for the bridegroom to return. Five of the virgins prepared for the coming by filling their lamps with oil, and five of them were foolish, having no oil. So when the bridegroom's coming was announced, the five foolish virgins were not ready. They ran to get oil in their lamps, but when they came back and knocked on the door, the bridegroom answered,

"Truly I say to you I do not know you." Jesus warns us in verse 13, "Be on the alert then, for you do not know the day nor the hour."

The Bible tells us that Christ will return like a thief in the night (Revelations 3:3 and 16:15). He could return on any day at any moment. It is possible that He could return today, and yet, would our lives be prepared to receive Him? I remember as a child thinking that I didn't want Jesus to come back until I had a chance to live my life, get married, and see the world. But I was foolish because I loved my life more than I loved Christ. Jesus said, "Whoever wishes to save his life will lose it; but whoever loses his life for My sake will find it" (Matthew 16:25).

Do you long for His coming? Do you anxiously seek the skies for His grand entrance? Do you feel the anticipation of His return in your heart or do you fear it?

My grandmother was a woman who lived her life in light of Christ's return. Her husband died when her three children were still very young. She never remarried, but instead she embraced a passion for Christ. She took her children to tent revivals all over the South in the 1960s, and they learned to minister even at ages as young as 8 years old, when my father preached his first sermon. To this day each of them still ministers through worship and the Word.

As a child, I saw my grandmother pacing the floor in prayer to Jesus. She rung her hands and prayed to Him aloud because she believed He was right there listening to her desperate cries for guidance and mercy (and He was). She continually talked of His coming and His love for her. To her, Jesus wasn't just a nice story; He was all that she had. She was very poor, a simple woman, but her Bible was worn from turned pages and notes scribbled in the margins.

When she died my aunt cleaned out boxes filled with notes she jotted down on scraps of paper, quotes she heard from sermons, scriptures that had special meaning—and they all pointed to one person—her Jesus.

She once wrote in a letter to me, "Forgive me for being so old. Of course, you'll never know what I mean because Jesus is coming back soon." She believed that I would not grow old like her because He would come before then … and she may be right! She taught me to look for Jesus in the clouds, as she often talked of His return and of heaven—her favorite song was "Acres of Diamonds," a melody that proclaimed the wonders of our eternal home.

Thoughts of Jesus were never far from her tongue. She knew Jesus, and He knew her. You could tell by the way she talked about Him and how His word ministered to her heart. She's in heaven now. He finally took her home to be with Him, and I know she's sitting with Him right now by the crystal sea, waiting for us to join her.

How do You Draw Near?

If you feel like Christ is not enough to fulfill you in your singleness, then perhaps you have never truly experienced His presence. To know Christ does not mean that feelings of loneliness suddenly disappear. We are all still waiting in anticipation for our Bridegroom, but we have been given a Comforter (John 14:16 KJV) and a promise of faith, so that we can have a relationship through the Spirit and a hope of His coming. Jesus said, "I stand at the door and knock" (Revelations 3:20). He is waiting for you to open the door of your heart so that you may become intimate with Him. James 4:8 says, "Draw near to God and He will draw near to you." Search your heart for a longing to be with Him. Do you really desire to know Christ? Are you ready for your life to be changed in a radical way? Too many Christians are comfortable with a mediocre relationship. The Bible promises when you seek Christ, you will find Him (Matthew 7:7, Luke 11:9).

Having an intimate relationship with Christ starts with a soft heart and a right attitude toward Him. If you truly want to go deeper spiritually, you must prepare your heart to meet with Him.

Start by confessing any unresolved sin in your heart. Even born again believers have sin in their lives. We all do things or have attitudes that we regret. Although sin will not take away a person's salvation, it can create a barrier in your intimacy with Christ. Guilt and shame have a way of destroying a relationship, but when you confess and repent, He is faithful to forgive you (1 John 1:9).

Make sure your confessions are specific. Don't use general statements like, "God forgive me for all the sins I committed today." But talk about precise moments, feelings, or attitudes. For example, say something like, "Lord, today when Stephanie was talking about her engagement, I confess that I was bitter toward her in my heart. I am so sorry, Father. Please put joy in my heart for her and her fiancé." By confessing, you are clearing the way to the heart of the Father by having an attitude of humility. As a result, you will feel the burden of sin lifted and a closer intimacy with Him.

Second, come to God with a humble heart, and ask Him to renew His Lordship in your life. If you have never received Christ as your personal Savior, see chapter 11 for more details on how to receive new life. But for those of us who are believers, we often still try to be in control of our own lives outside of God's calling. If you have found yourself directing what you think is best for your life instead of relying on God, then humbly ask Him to give you the heart of a servant and give up fighting for control of your life.

Allowing Jesus to be Lord means that you are no longer trying to find a way to force your agenda on Him, but you are actively yielding to seek and obey His will, no matter how fearful you are of the journey. It's an act of faith and trust as you face situations, like loneliness, that you might never have chosen for yourself.

Third, become like a child. In Matthew 18:3, Jesus says, "Unless you … become like children, you will not enter the kingdom of heaven." Do you remember being a child? Children simply believe what they are told. They learn and follow and trust the ones that love and care for them.

For most people, childhood is a carefree stage of life. There are no dreams that are off limits to children. When I was a little girl, I wanted to be a dancer. I would dress up in a flowing dress and practice even through I never took lessons. I didn't look at myself in the mirror and said, "What are you doing? You'll never be a dancer!" I simply believed I would be. Some dreams survive; some fade away, but children live on a day to day contentment of tomorrow's dreams.

The Bible calls that kind of hopeful belief "faith." Hebrews 11:1 describes faith as the "substance of things hoped for, the evidence of things not seen" (NKJV). In other words to have faith is to act upon something, even without seeing the physical evidence. With Christ, we have the same hope. We have never seen Jesus with our eyes, but we have a promise, and the Spirit bares witness that He is indeed the Messiah. We have never seen heaven even though the Bible calls us "citizens." We are told that in this world we are aliens and strangers. Our home is a mystery to us. But we have been told many wonderful things about it—no more tears, no more pain, no more sorrow.

What soldier doesn't dream about his home with fond memories and hopes of being there again one day? Although his life is in danger, he has faith that he will make it back there, and in the meantime the hope of home sustains him in the battle. It is the same for Christians. The more we think about our home, the more we long for it.

When was the last time you thought about heaven? After the death of my first husband, I thought about it more than ever before. Why not stop and think about it right now—What it will be like? What will you do? Who will you see? As for me, I've always imaged a special place next to the bank of a small river underneath a shade tree. What about you? What would you imagine your special heavenly place to be like?

The next time you feel lonely and weary from your battles in this life, think of heaven, think of eternity, and remember your Bridegroom. As you wait for His physical return, you are not without His company, so take advantage of the blessings that come while you wait for Him.

Overcoming Obstacles

In this book, we have covered six blessings of loneliness—sacrifice, suffering, brokenness, dying to self, service, and waiting for the bridegroom. None of these six are easy. They require a lot of prayer, dependence upon God, and fighting the innate self focus that comes with the sinful nature of all flesh. But more than anything else, they require that we live by what Jesus calls the two greatest commandments: love God with all your heart, soul, mind, and strength and love your neighbor has yourself (Luke 10:27).

As believers any of us would say that we love God first and foremost, but do we live that way? If we love God more than anything else in the world, then we will want to please Him with our lives, seeking to obey His will. We have already discovered that God desires great and beautiful things for each of our lives individually, even if that means we must walk through suffering (Jeremiah 29:11). In seeking His will above anything else you not only find purpose through your loneliness, but you are guaranteed to find the right path through life.

In addition, we are promised His love, joy, peace, patience, kindness, gentleness, goodness, faithfulness, and self-control, instead of bitterness, frustration, and chaos. And when we go through sacrifice or suffering or brokenness for the sake of following Christ, we are not left with the residue of our hurt, but we find grace, healing, and strength in the wake of these tidal waves.

Second, in order to experience the blessings of loneliness, you must learn to love others as you love yourself. Dying to self, sacrifice, service … these are actions that are not possible without a genuine love for others. It's so important to be active in others' lives and to reach out to other singles. This love in action not only validates our faith to onlookers and glorifies God, it also often validates a stronger belief in our own hearts, giving purpose to our lives.

James 2:26 tells us that faith without works is dead. In other words, to say that you glorify God and that you love others does no good unless you show your love for God and man through actions. James 2:15-18 puts it best:

If a brother or sister is without clothing and in need of daily food, and one of you says to them, 'Go in peace, be warmed and be filled,' and yet you do not give them what is necessary for their body, what use is that? Even so faith, if it has no works, is dead, being by itself.

To love God and to love others are difficult concepts for anyone to grasp, simply because humans are beings of both flesh and spirit, and those different parts of us war with each other (Galatians 15:16-18). But it is important that we keep battling the fleshly urge to live for our own desires, to serve ourselves, to make our lives the center of our world, and instead seek the will of God.

Galatians 6:7b-9 promises, "…Whatever a man sows, this he will also reap. For the one who sows to his own flesh will from the flesh reap corruption, but the one who sows to the Spirit will from the Spirit reap eternal life. Let us not lose heart in doing good, for in due time we will reap if we do not grow weary."

In the lifestyle of Christian singles there are three main obstacles that often get in the way of loving others and glorifying God, and they are envy and jealousy, isolation, and sexual temptation. Each of these obstacles keeps singles from loving others around them with a Christ-like love and block the blessings that have been discussed in this book. In the next three chapters, I am going to address these stumbling blocks and give you some suggestions on how to overcome them.

In addition, chapter 11 gives an explanation of the gospel of Jesus Christ. If you are reading this book and have not come to know God's saving grace, you will not be able to experience the blessings of loneliness until you have. A relationship with Christ is the only way to comprehend and apply these principles. Without it, nothing—not marriage, money, status, or benevolence—will satisfy your loneliness.

Humans were created as spiritual beings, and as it has been said, there is a "God-sized hole in each one of us." Only Christ can fill that gap. Not Buddha, not Muhammad, not Confucius. Only Jesus. If you are not a believer, let me encourage you to read this chapter to learn how you can have a personal relationship with the God of the universe—He is the only One who can bring peace, joy, love, and hope to your life, but without Jesus we can do nothing (John 15:5). If you are a believer, I want to encourage you also to read that chapter. Not only will it encourage your own faith, but it will also give you the tools that you need to lead others to Christ as you walk through the blessings of loneliness and share His love and blessings with them.

Chapter 8

Overcoming Jealousy and Envy

*"For where jealousy and selfish ambition exist, there is disorder and
every evil thing."*

-James 3:16

My boyfriend and I had only been broken up for a short while, and I
had hopes that we were on the road to reconciliation. Despite our
differences, things seemed to be going better than they had in the past. We
were spending more quality time together, and we were working out a lot
of our differences through better communication. Then one day he called
and said he wanted to stop seeing me altogether.

I was crushed. I couldn't figure out what had gone wrong. I thought
he was my very best friend. He was the one that I saw when I dreamed
about the future. I didn't know how I would survive without him in my
life.

It was the Christmas season, and we hadn't talked in several days.
Some of the singles from church were hosting a white elephant party. I
walked in alone and immediately scanned the room to see if my ex-
boyfriend was there. About 30 singles stood in a circle around the dining
room table exchanging gifts. The house seemed devoid of his presence, so
I took my place in the perimeter of the group.

Then out of the corner of my eye, I saw him. Of course, he was
standing next to the newest prettiest girl in the group. Her long blonde
hair and China-doll complexion made me feel so plain. He talked and
laughed with her, seemingly oblivious to my existence. They chatted and

giggled the way two people attracted to each other do—those nervous yet poised bits of laughter, coupled with glances from soft eyes.

As I watched them, jealousy came over me like a fever, boiling blood rising up within me. I tried to ignore and pretend to have a good time, but I was completely captivated by the two lovebirds.

I became so jealous that no matter where I looked, my vision was literally blurred. The only exception was when I focused on the flirting, carefree couple—no matter how distorted the rest of the room seemed, there was always a perfectly clear oval of vision around them.

Inside I was screaming, "Why? This isn't fair! *I* should be with him!" My jealousy fumed against this woman whom I had only recently met. I tried to shake the thoughts out of my mind, but my feelings consumed me, and I had no idea what to do about it. I sucked in the tears, but the expression on my face exposed my undeniable rage.

I made a fool out of myself by the end of the evening because I just couldn't keep my mind off of what was going on, yet I refused to leave. I didn't want to go, not knowing what was happening between them. The night ended in desperate tears as my ex refused to talk to me about the situation.

That was just the beginning of my bouts with extreme jealousy and envy during the next two years as my ex-boyfriend dated different girls within that timeframe. I had battled with these emotions most of my life in one form or another, but they were never more intense than during this period. I suffered greatly with jealousy and envy, but eventually God brought me through this terrible emotional plague. It wasn't until I was able to overcome these feelings that I could receive of the blessings of loneliness.

Jealousy and Envy *can* be Defeated

Genesis 4:5-8 tells us the story of the famous brothers Cain and Abel, whose lives were destroyed by jealousy and envy. During the Old Testament times, God demanded a burnt sacrifice from men to cover their sins. Abel was a shepherd, so he sacrificed a lamb, and Cain was a harvester, so he burnt bundles of wheat as his sacrifice. God accepted Abel's sacrifice, but He was not pleased with Cain's.

As a result, Cain became very angry at God's rejection of him. Cain was jealous of God's love—he thought it was his right to have it. And at the same time he was envious of his brother. So God said to Cain, "Why are you angry, Cain? And why has your countenance fallen? If you do well, will not your countenance be lifted up? And if you do not do well, sin is crouching at the door; and its desire is for you, *but you must master it*" (Genesis 4:6-7, emphasis added).

Through God's statement to Cain, two things are made clear. First, jealousy and envy can turn into sin if they are not mastered, and second, but most importantly, *they can be mastered.* Just like God instructed Cain, we must also master our jealousy and envy. Otherwise, we will end up with bitterness in our hearts as Cain did. That's not to say that everyone who feels these emotions will eventually murder his opponent and be cursed by God like Cain, but bitterness will hurt in other ways. It might come out in hurting others emotionally or harming yourself in some way. No matter what the outcome, though, not dealing with bitterness in the heart caused by jealousy and envy is a dangerous condition.

The Difference Between Jealousy and Envy

Although these emotions are very similar, there is a difference between the two. Jealousy occurs when you already possess something and don't wish to share it with anyone else. You want to keep it for yourself. In my case, I was jealous of my ex-boyfriend because in my mind, the relationship I had with him *should* be mine, and I didn't want to share that with any other girl.

Wanting to have a relationship is not wrong—we all want to love and be loved. Sharon A. Hersh, author of the book *Brave Hearts* says, "The roots of jealousy reveal the holy longings for relationships that God has written in our hearts." [8] Even God describes Himself as jealous. Exodus 34:14 says, "...you shall not worship any other god, for the Lord, whose name is Jealous, is a jealous God." God does not desire to share our affections with any other god—He wants our love all to Himself.

Jealousy becomes a problem for someone who is single when there is really no relationship to hold on to. It's also a problem when the jealousy empowers you to hold on to a relationship in order to maintain control. I struggled with this. I was no longer dating this person, but in my mind, he was still *my* boyfriend. I believed that I could win him back, so I had a hard time letting go, even though this was not the person God had for me.

The book of James explains the kind of evil jealousy that can destroy. "If you have bitter jealousy and selfish ambition in your heart, do not be arrogant and so lie against the truth. This wisdom is not that which comes down from above, but is earthly, natural, demonic. For where jealousy and selfish ambition exist, there is disorder and every evil thing" (3:13-16).

Envy is slightly different. This occurs when you see something that someone else has, like a relationship, and you want it for yourself. In the world of singles, this is what occurs when you see a friend dating someone, getting married, etc., and then you covet her circumstances.

The problem in this situation comes when you allow envy to make you believe that another person's gifts, life situations, or abilities are better than what God has given you. This mindset makes us act in negative ways toward others and embitters our hearts, which is where sin comes in.

Combatting Jealousy

Have you found yourself in a situation of jealousy like mine? I believed in my mind that my ex-boyfriend should be with me, not another girl. I felt like I had the rights to his love, even though reality proved that I did not have any rights to a relationship with him. The fact was we had broken up.

If you have found yourself in this situation, you must begin to let go of the relationship. The first thing you need to do is *address your fears*. Jealousy results when you fear losing something. In my situation, I knew the girl at the Christmas party was pretty and sweet, and I was afraid that I would "lose" my ex-boyfriend to her.

Dr. Dan Allender, counselor and author of *Cry of the Soul*, says that jealousy comes from a form of fear—the fear of being alone—and putting our faith in a relationship instead of God to fulfill us. He says, "All wrong jealousy is the utter fear. [It's the thought that says,] 'I'm going to be abandoned. And in the abandonment I am going to be desolate and alone in a way where I will not be able to survive. So you are my god. You must somehow stay with me and be my fullness and therefore be my false god.'" [9] These fears may include not getting married, not finding a suitable mate, being alone, or facing rejection. Let me suggest that you make a list of the things you fear, and ask God to give you strength to put your faith in Him, and not worry about these uncertainties.

As we talked about earlier in the book, fear is the opposite of faith. Do you believe that God is in control of your circumstances? Do you believe that He causes all things to work together for good (Romans 8:28)? You must be willing to trust God's will and follow it, even if it means letting go of and losing a relationship. Job 1:21 says, "[God] gives, He takes, and He does no injustice." God knows what's best for you, even when you don't know yourself. Could it be that the reason you are losing this relationship is actually for your own good?

Trusting God also involves recognizing that you are not in control of your life. Have you found yourself trying to make your own destiny come true? Have you tried forcing relationships that don't seem to work? If you find yourself in these situations, you are trying to control your future, but you cannot take the place of God. Why would you want to? If He has all wisdom and all knowledge; if He is purely good, and He knows all things to come, then why wouldn't you trust Him? Instead of panicking when unpleasant circumstances befall you, ask God to show you the reasons why you are going through these circumstances. You will find that there is always a purpose for everything we endure.

I was just talking to a single friend the other day who recently went through a break up. As we talked, I tried to encourage her by explaining that she will find her fulfillment if she accepts her singleness and finds contentment where she is. She replied, "I feel like God has called me to be a wife and a mother and to have a family, and *that* is what will fulfill me."

Had God called her to be a wife and a mother? Perhaps. Who am I to judge another person's calling? But I *can* justify this thought—if God wanted her to be married with children right now, and if He wanted this relationship to work out, it would have. Period. God is the one in control of our destinies, not us. She can trust Him to fulfill His promises, so why not take advantage of the time He's given her right now for His purposes?

When you begin to see the reasons and the lessons for your circumstances, you will start to understand the necessity of losing this relationship, and you will no longer be jealous of other women that he talks to. You will understand that you do not have "rights" over his life, and that God has destined for you to be apart. As you see the purpose for your singleness it will give you confidence in God's work.

Combatting Envy

Envy is probably more universal among singles. I don't think I've known a single who hasn't struggle with envy, particularly when it comes to desiring a relationship like his or her friends. As we mentioned earlier, envy is the act of wanting something that you don't have, something that you see in someone else's life. Envy comes from a combination of two actions: Comparison and a lack of gratitude.

Comparison is the act of measuring another person's commodities, whether internal or external, and judging, *based on your own impressions*, as to which is better. Most of the time what you have pales in comparison to what someone else has. As the old saying goes, "The grass is always greener on the other side of the fence."

In 2 Corinthians 10:12, the Apostle Paul uses the example of false teachers in the church to show how comparison is unwise. He says, "For we are not bold to class or compare ourselves with some of those who commend themselves; but when they measure themselves by themselves and compare themselves with themselves, they are without understanding."

It's easy to look at a couple that is married or dating and compare your happiness with theirs. You may be envious because you long for what they have in a relationship. You want companionship, and they seem to have that. You long for acceptance, and they seem to have that. You believe that a relationship would cure your loneliness, and they seemingly have discovered that cure.

The problem is you have forgotten that God has a unique destiny for *you*. You haven't seen what He has planned for you in the future, and you haven't seen what He has planned for *that* couple. The happiness you seek will come as you purpose to fulfill God's calling in your life, whether it comes through marriage or not.

The other problem of comparison is that the focus falls completely on yourself—either trying to achieve what you don't have or by wallowing in self pity over what you don't have. This keeps you from loving others and having compassion. Biblical counselor David Powlison writes powerfully about this kind of thinking:

101

It might manifest as subtly as spending an unnecessary extra couple of minutes in front of the mirror trying to fix what is unacceptable ... or stewing internally in regrets and "if onlys." Mental or actual tinkering with appearance can chew up amazing amounts of time and energy. Or perhaps upon walking into the fellowship hall after church, a woman is instantly aware of what every other woman is wearing, and has sized up how she compares. Her very gaze at other people is conditioned to a status hierarchy defined by images of beauty, and thus to the attendant jealousy self-loathing, competitiveness, inferiority/superiority comparisons, and the like. Perhaps she obsessively pursues alterations in her appearance: hair color, weight loss, new clothing, makeup, cosmetic operations. Perhaps she slides into an "eating disorder." Perhaps she plunges into despair and gives up, gaining 100 pounds, becoming unkempt, "uglifying" herself. "'I'm a failure" simply registers a different manifestation of devotion to the lie. All such preoccupations rob her of the joy and freedom of faith in Christ the Lord, and sap energies that might be spent in loving concern for others. [10]

Comparison is not the only problem of envy; it is coupled with ungratefulness. When we compare ourselves to someone else, we become discontent with what God has given us. His gifts no longer seem gracious but rather less than adequate. Comparison makes us believe that God's gifts are not good enough.

When my missionary friend, Tammy, was overseas, conditions weren't good. They didn't have the plush American life that they were used to, including toilets that didn't work and sleeping conditions that were uncomfortable. She and the other missionaries would play a game called "It Could Be Worse." They would make up these terrible conditions that they *could be* living in. These stories of worse conditions would make them laugh, but also made their situation look a lot better, causing them to be grateful for what they did have.

How long has it been since you thanked God for the blessings of loneliness? It might be something as simple as "I'm grateful for my own bed" or something as deep as "I'm grateful that I can use this time to deepen my walk with Christ." Take a few moments right now to write down a list of all the things you appreciate about being single. It may be difficult at first, but keep the list with you so you can add things as you think of them. Then on days when you find yourself envious of your married friends, take out your list and remind yourself of all the blessings that come with being single.

How to Overcome

Jealousy and envy are not hopeless conditions. You do not have to live your life carrying these burdens, which can cause divisions and separations in your church and in your spiritual walk. We are the Body of Christ, and we are called to unity. Galatians 5:25-26 says, "If we live by the Spirit, let us also walk by the Spirit. Let us not become boastful, challenging one another, envying one another."

It's important that you commit to battling against these vices to get rid of their existence in your heart, not only for unity of the body but also so you might receive the blessings that come from defeating them.

It begins with a right perspective of yourself. This is not so much a matter of having *self*-esteem but having confidence in Christ, who lives *in* and *through* you. Every gift that we possess comes to us by the grace of God (James 1:17), including the gift of being single and, yes, even the gift of loneliness. You must remember that we are nothing and deserve nothing, but because of Christ, we have life and joy and peace.

Each of us is given a unique destiny, and one is not better than the other. Paul said, "Not that I speak from want, for I have learned to be content in whatever circumstances I am" (Philippians 4:11). Like Paul, learn to accept where God has allowed you to be. He created you and formed you for a specific purpose in life, and it has been uniquely formed for you. The same is true for the other person of whom you are jealous or envious. Each individual in the Body of Christ is like a puzzle piece. Each of us has a different part in completing the puzzle. If all of the pieces of the puzzle were the same, then none of us would fit together. But because we are all different and individually designed, each of us has a special place in making the whole picture come together.

God will call some to marriage and others will be called to singleness. It's not a matter of whose calling is better, but of how well you fulfill the calling you have been given.

All of God's plans are good, and we need to realize what our destiny is and fulfill it. You must have faith that His will is better than your own, and you would be wise to seek His, not yours. When you embrace your own destiny and pursue it without looking for other things to fulfill you, you will no longer have a place for jealousy and envy in your heart, and you will learn what it means to be content.

You must also have a right perspective of others. No one is perfect, and no one has everything all together in life. Every person in the world has problems from time to time. Just because the person you admire appears to have the "perfect" life or exist in what you would call "ideal" circumstances, you have no idea what is going on under the surface of her heart. It may be that you would not choose to have a life like hers if you knew what was going on behind the façade. As you look at others around you, don't be deceived by believing that you are the only one who is hurting. As you take the focus off of yourself and put it onto others you will start to see the pain inside people and no longer feel alone in your distress.

Also, keep the perspective that we are called to love one another and to carry each other's burdens. When you have compassion for another person, it's not easy to hold bitterness against him or her. Galatians 6:2-4 says, "Bear one another's burdens, and thereby fulfill the law of Christ. For if anyone thinks he is something when he is nothing, he deceives himself. But each one must examine his own work, and then he will have reason for boasting in regard to himself alone, and not in regard to another."

The Christian community was set up by God to be a family that takes care of each other. Galatians 5:13-15 says,

> *For you were called to freedom, brethren; only do not turn your freedom into an opportunity for the flesh, but through love, serve one another. For the whole law is fulfilled in one word, in the statement, "You shall love your neighbor as yourself." But if you bite and devour one another, take care that you are not consumed by one another.*

Allowing jealousy to settle in your heart will cause bitterness and from there biting and devouring. This is the kind of self-consumption Paul talks about in Romans 14:10-13:

But you, why do you judge your brother? Or you again, why do you regard your brother with contempt? For we will all stand before the judgment seat of God. For it is written, "As I live, says the Lord, every knee shall bow to me, and every tongue shall give praise to God." So then each one of us will give an account of himself to God. Therefore let us not judge one another anymore, but rather determine this—not to put an obstacle or a stumbling block in a brother's way.

Last, begin the process of healing. To begin, you must pray to God and confess that your jealousy and envy is sin. This is an important process because it cleanses the heart. By confessing, you can no longer say, "I'm jealous for good reason." Now, you have recognized it as sin and you can no longer justify it, forcing you to take responsibility for your transgression, and now you can reconcile it. If you keep putting the blame on the other person for your jealousy and envy, then you will never rid yourself of this plague.

The next step in this process is to confess your sin to anyone you have offended because of it. If you have reacted from your envy in ways that were not appropriate (for instance, making sarcastic comments, disrespecting, or any other form of hurt) then you should confess your envy and ask for forgiveness from that person. If the envy you felt was not detected by that person, it isn't necessary to confess to her. If you did, that might actually cause resentment instead of reconciliation.

When you have cleared your heart, begin to spend time with her. It's not necessary to be best friends, but when you have a chance, hold a conversation. Talk about something deeper than the normal surface conversations. Ask questions about her life and her struggles. You will see that she is a person just like you, fallacies and all.

I did this with one young lady that I envied. I never really got to know her previously because I counted her as an enemy. I was resentful because she was a close friend to a guy that I was interested in, and I was afraid they would begin dating. I knew that the sin was mine, and I determined to overcome it.

At a party one night, I saw her sitting alone. I knew there were many of her friends there, so I had compassion on her, not knowing why she was so alone. I went over and struck up a conversation and found out that she was actually going through a very difficult time at the moment. She opened up to me, telling me about her situation, and I was able to give her some advice from my own experiences. After that, I felt comfortable around her and the awkwardness was no longer there. My heart was at peace because I could see that she was a person who needed compassion—she was someone like me.

All this time I had suffered with the awkwardness of seeing her and being in her company, but all of it was completely unnecessary. When the sin was purged from my heart, that rift in the Body of Christ was healed and there was peace. I no longer had to carry the burden of twisted feelings and tension in my body. I wish I hadn't waited so long.

Hebrews 12:14 tells us to "seek to be at peace with all men." Is it possible to have peace with everyone in life? No, but it is possible to *seek* it, even when the issues that divide us carry over for years. Let me give you an example of what I mean. I had harbored resentment against another girl, and before I could reconcile, I moved and didn't see her anymore. A year or two later, she moved near me, and we started running into each other frequently.

I was amazed that although I was married at this time and no longer had a reason to be jealous of an ex-boyfriend, I still associated those feelings with this person each time I saw her. I wasn't sure if I should just ignore her or try to pray away the awkward feeling. Finally, the Lord told me that I needed to resolve the issue and seek to be at peace with her in my heart, so I took her out to lunch. We caught up on our lives and chatted and shared, and when I really got to know her, I was no longer intimidated. We were at peace.

Jealousy and envy are problems, even when they seem small, like my situation with the girl I took to lunch. Don't allow Satan to convince you that the jealousy is not your fault or that your feelings are incurable. Christ will give you the strength to reconcile, and you will be able to receive more purely the blessings of loneliness when you overcome in this area.

Chapter 9

Overcoming Isolation

"In God I have put my trust, I shall not be afraid. What
can man do to me?"
-Psalm 56:11

Shelly was a beautiful girl, and she looked like she had it all together. She was physically fit and youthful, successful at her job and very talented. But Shelly was also very lonely.

"The loneliness was almost overwhelming," she told me. "I knew I needed to be with other people, but I was afraid."

Even though Shelly had all the outward appearances of someone who was confident, she had a problem that stood in the way of finding the blessings of her loneliness—she was afraid of what people thought of her.

For months this fear kept her indoors, sitting alone in her apartment, eating alone, working alone. She came and went day after day without friends because she was terrified to reach out. Eventually, the solitude became so great that Shelly knew she must do something. "It was either face my fear or die from loneliness," she said, "so I decided to reach out and live."

Shelly discovered a very important concept in the world—loneliness is devastating when you isolate yourself. In order to receive the blessings that come from loneliness, it is imperative that you spend time with people. You can't serve others when there is no one in your life to serve. You can't have compassion for others when there is no one to understand.

You can't share the burdens of others when there is no one to listen to. And so the purpose you seek is waiting for you in the faces of the crowd.

What Causes Isolation

What caused Shelley to stay far away from people? What was she really afraid of? Shelly wasn't afraid that someone was going to jump out and attack her physically. She wasn't afraid that people might give her a contagious deadly illness. It was really a fear of rejection.

Whether the fear of men comes from insecurity or from past experiences of rejection, singles often purposely put up walls to shut out relationships. These are people who have believed the lie that it is easier to resist pain and live life without showing hurt than it is to face it. Sheri Rose Shepherd, a former Miss America and author of *My Prince Will Come*, wrote, "Loneliness [or isolation] is often rooted in selfishness or the fear of getting hurt. It is truly beautiful to watch people who have learned the art of loving one another." The isolated individual may vow in her heart, "No one will ever hurt me again!" But choosing that path will only cause the pain to become more self-indulgent and reach much deeper into the soul. It reminds me of the old Simon and Garfunkel song, "I Am a Rock."

Don't talk of love
Well I've heard the word before
It's sleeping in my memory
I won't disturb the slumber
Of feelings that have died
If I never loved I never would have cried

I am a rock
I am an island

I have my books
And my poetry to protect me
I am shielded in my armor
Hiding in my room

Safe within my womb
I touch no one and no one touches me

I am a rock
I am an island...

And a rock feels no pain
And an island never cries[11]

But rocks are hard and impenetrable and islands are isolated—a high price to pay for a painless life. When you're in the mindset of self-preservation, everyone falls second to your own feelings, including God. You convince yourself that you won't be vulnerable. You won't show a weakness. That way, no one will ever hurt you again. When you have these thoughts, you are really saying to yourself, "I don't care about anyone else. The most important thing in my life is me. I am going to keep from getting hurt, even if it means I have to hurt other people to protect myself."

The more you think of yourself, the more others don't matter. You start believing, "They should be worried about *my* hurts, *my* feelings, *my* needs!" In a sense, your own feelings become an idol—you succumb to their desires, and your feelings control your life.

Overcoming Isolation

Can I share a secret with you? I am afraid of people, too. The fear of rejection can be paralyzing at times. I want to be liked by everyone, but something inside me says, "You're not likeable. Look at you—you're not fun; you're a lousy conversationalist. Nobody listens to you anyway, so why bother talking? You're so strange—no one could ever understand the way you are." Sometimes, I don't even want to answer the phone because I'm afraid I might say the wrong thing and cause someone to be mad at me. I often won't say someone's name because I'm so worried I might get the name wrong and offend him or her. It's a life-consuming fear.

It's thoughts like these that make me want to live in isolation. A friend of mine and I have a joke—when we're tired of dealing with people and with life, we ask the other if she's ready to move to Montana, in the mountains far away from everyone. It would be very easy to avoid all these fears by avoiding people—just stay inside my safe four walls most of the time, only making one or two friends, stop being active in church, always look down and avoid eye contact. For someone with my personality, I could easily adjust to that lifestyle. But then I wouldn't be able to serve others, help others, and most of all love others, like Jesus has shown His followers to do.

It's not that my fears are unfounded; there is a lot of truth in them. As a child, I felt rejected because my family was poor, and kids can be cruel. I actually *have* said things that unintentionally hurt feelings. There have been times when I *have* been a lousy conversationalist. But like everything, Satan has taken these truths and twisted them into "always" statements. The logic seems reasonable, but reality is not truly reflected. 2 Corinthians 11:14 says, "Satan disguises himself as an angel of light." What this means is that when you see him, he appears to be one of the good guys—like an angel. But he is a deceiver, also referred to as "the father of lies" (John 8:44).

Sheri Rose Shepherd describes how isolation is exactly what Satan needs to destroy us. "The enemy of our soul loves it when we [isolate ourselves]. In fact, he tries to separate us from other people. That is one of his most important and often unrecognized strategies. When a lion is hungry, the king of beasts doesn't go after the whole herd. He can't defeat a herd, and he doesn't even try. Instead, he goes after an isolated animal. Likewise, the devil tries to separate an unsuspecting victim from the body of believers. His goal is to isolate the weak, and he sees past the pained smile on our face. We might as well paint a bull's-eye on our chest and say, 'Come and get me, Satan! I'm alone.'" [12]

God created us to be a family, and a family cannot function if the members are torn apart. Cissy, a single who has struggled with this in the past, said, "I tended to isolate myself. It was a defense I used to tell myself that I didn't need anyone, and it became a trap to rely on self and make me walk in pride. But I found that God really works in relationships—all kinds. So I have to submit to God daily and remember that the purpose of my life is to have relationships with others and to do the will of God."

God created the Church to be that family where relationships take place, so your first step in overcoming isolation is to learn to be an active member of the Body of Christ. That may mean seeking out a local singles group at a church. If your church doesn't have one, many larger churches will allow you to attend their group even if you're a member somewhere else.

You may also decide to *start* a singles group at your church. If this project seems too large for you, invite a few close friends to join you each week for fellowship, Bible study, and prayer time.

We are told in Hebrews 10:25 not to stop meeting with one another as believers, and I believe that it is particularly important that Christian singles gather together. A group of friends provides a warm atmosphere, understanding, safety, accountability, and strength when you are weak. Many singles live far from their relatives, and a group of Christian friends can become a kind of family. It also promotes healthy interaction between members of the opposite sex. Men and women can grow from the strengths of the other as they relate with godly manners and conduct.

It is important that you not only attend church and other social activities with Christian friends but that you share your gifts with that body of believers. Do you have musical abilities? Then join the worship team. Perhaps God has given you the desire to work with children. Then volunteer for Sunday school or work in the nursery. You could be on the welcoming committee (which can help you overcome a lot of fears) or even lead a small group.

If insecurity keeps you from reaching out, first remember that loving begins with dying. Disregard what people think of you and be the person God made you to be. The truth is that God created your personality exactly as He desired it to be (Psalm 139:13). You have value in God's eyes, and He has placed gifts in you that no one else can offer. Remember the words of 1 John 4:4, "You are from God, little children, and have overcome them; because greater is He who is in you than he who is in the world."

The Bible tells us that we are not to fear man but God. You shouldn't be so concerned about what others think of you, but instead consider how God sees you live your life. The psalmist David wrote in Psalm 56:11, "In God I have put my trust, I shall not be afraid. What can man do to me?" You see, when you are pleasing God by loving Him and loving others in your life, then men are powerless. You don't need the acceptance of men when you realize that you are already accepted in Christ. He loves you and receives you and calls you just as you are, mistakes and all.

Getting Beyond the Fear

If you have a hard time getting beyond your fear of people like Shelly and me, here are some ways to help you begin to open up again.

First, remember that the strength to reach out beyond yourself comes from Christ. I John 4:7-8 says, "Beloved, let us love one another, for love is from God; and everyone who loves is born of God and knows God. The one who does not love does not know God, for God is love." Love comes from God, so if you know Him personally, the love for others already exists in your heart. As you die to yourself, the love of God will fill your life, and will overflow onto others around you. You have not been asked to do anything that God has not equipped you to do. As Philippians 4:13 says, "I can do all things through Him who strengthens me."

Second, develop close friendships with just one or two people of the same gender. When you go to a church gathering, meet one or two people and ask them to go with you to the movies or out to dinner. You won't start off as best friends, but as you begin to develop memories together, you will see your friendships blossom and grow. When you have conversations, don't just talk about what you did that day or your plans for the weekend, but open up about who you are. Share your joys and your struggles. Ask questions and talk about your own spiritual walk. As a result, you will begin to form deep friendships and instead of feeling afraid when you enter the doors of the sanctuary, you can look forward to friendly faces.

Let me also emphasize that it's important that these singles be your same gender. If you are a woman, do not develop these kinds of friendships with men, and vice versa. Developing these kinds of close friendships with the opposite sex is a recipe for romance. Don't get me wrong—there's nothing wrong with having friends of the opposite gender, but when your goal is to overcome isolation and reach out, it's best to make solid friendships that have the potential to last a lifetime. It also eliminates the possibility of a broken heart, which can only further your fear of rejection and cause more pain.

Last, if you are not a part of a singles group at church, ask your news friends to go with you to check it out. Singles groups can be very intimidating to attend alone, but going with a friend can build up confidence. It's important to be with other Christian singles who are also facing similar struggles. You can find some answers for the loneliness you face, and you will also find comfort knowing that you're not going through difficult situations alone. In addition, the social atmosphere is safe and offers many opportunities to get involved.

If you have been going to church, but have not been active, the next time there is a meeting, commit to meet someone new while you're there. Don't wait for someone to introduce himself or herself to you. I remember the first outing I went on with my singles group. I was standing near another guy, and I kept wondering why he didn't introduce himself to me. Finally, I walked up to him and said, "Hi, my name is Sabrina. I'm new here." In reply he said, "Hi, my name is Jeff. I'm new myself. This is my second time to visit." You see, he was brand new just like I was, but I had assumed that he was being standoffish. Little did I know that he was thinking the same thing about me! Next time you go to an event, take the risk and be the first to reach out.

Rejection of man is really nothing to fear. As Psalm 118:6 says, "The Lord is for me; I will not fear; what can man do to me?" And Romans 8:31 echoes that feeling with these words from the Apostle Paul, "What then shall we say to these things? If God is for us, who is against us?" Once you reach out and start to experience what it's like to love others with your heart and die to self, I guarantee that you will one day wonder why you were so afraid. Satan would have you think that "no one likes you" but it isn't true. When you take the time to love others, they can't help but love you in return. Proverbs 18:24 (KJV) says, "A man that hath friends must shew himself friendly." People love people who love them first. And when you love others with the love of God, then you will no longer be afraid of them. As 1 John 4:18 teaches us, "There is no fear in love; but perfect love casts out fear, because fear involves punishment, and the one who fears is not perfected in love." When you love, you no longer have anything to fear because the welfare of the other person is more important than yourself.

Today, follow Shelly's example—decide to reach out and live … and in the process you will overcome isolation.

Chapter 10

Overcoming Sexual Temptation

"Whatever is true, whatever is honorable, whatever is right, whatever is pure, whatever is lovely, whatever is of good repute, if there is any excellence and if anything worthy of praise, dwell on these things."
-Philippians 4:8

"You know this doesn't mean anything," my ex-boyfriend said. In a moment alone, he kissed me, and he knew that I wanted him to.

"Yes," I replied, but deep inside I hoped that it did mean something. I hoped that if he held me in his arms again that he would remember how much he missed me. I wanted to be loved and accepted even if only for a little while.

And there we sat for the next hour kissing passionately, yet with a clear pact that it was all empty passion. Although there was no "sex," there was plenty of sin. Normally, I would have never done such a thing, but it was all for the hope of belonging. I was lonely, and I wanted to feel like someone wanted me, even if I had to allow sin.

Feeling lonely is a powerful tool for sexual temptation. To be tempted is not wrong. Because we were born with a sin nature, all of us have a desire to do the things of the world. Sin happens when you act upon those lusts, even if you act upon them only in your heart. James 1:14, 15 says, "But each one is tempted when he is carried away and enticed by his own lust. Then when lust has conceived, it gives birth to sin; and when sin is accomplished, it brings forth death."

In addition, sexual *desires* are not wrong. Those desires are actually necessary for both procreation and the enrichment of the marriage relationship. The problem is that they are only good and right in God's eyes when they are exercised in the bonds of matrimony. Sex is the only activity in the Bible that is a sin when you are *not* married and a blessing when you *are.*

In their book *Sexual Intimacy in Marriage*, William Cutrer and Sandra Glahn explain, "As with any of God's good gifts, sexuality—created as a wonderful expression of covenant love and intimate bonding—can become a painful trap and a seemingly irresistible force. Its immense power finds its full expression within marriage—a committed, covenant relationship. When people seek sexual pleasure devoid of commitment, accountability, and responsibility for personal actions, they often find themselves in a downward spiral of self-destruction"

That means that any sexual activity outside of marriage is a sin—that includes oral sex, heavy petting, and passionate kissing. Shannon Etheridge, author of *Every Young Woman's Battle*, wrote, "Although [women who practice these activities] may be virgins (medically speaking), they are *not* sexually pure. One can be a physical virgin but a mental, emotional, and spiritual prostitute."

So what is the lonely single to do with God-given sexual desires? Did God give these desires to torture singles? There is nothing more soothing than the loving touch of another human, especially when you have felt undesired for so long. A woman was widowed more than 30 years ago and never remarried. She was closest to her daughter and son, but both of them were married. One night when her son's wife was out of town, she came over and spent the evening with him. As they watched a movie together, the son gently pat her hair and held her hand. Before going home, she turned and said to him, "You're the only one who touches me anymore. It feels good to be touched." It wasn't a sexual longing, but it was a desire to be loved and to receive physical affection. If these desires cannot be fulfilled then why did God give them?

In the booklet *Singled Out for Him,* Nancy Leigh DeMoss describes the reasons for unfulfilled longings. She says, "All of us long for security and a certain level of creature comforts. Sometimes God is pleased to provide far more than we actually need. But sometimes He allows us to do without—to experience unfulfilled longings—so that we might come to recognize our need for Him."

As you face these sexual temptations or the need for human affection, allow them to push you toward God. Galatians 5:16 says, "Walk in the Spirit, and you will not carry out the desire of the flesh." As discussed earlier, this life is only temporary. There is no marriage or sex in heaven. This life is only a preparation for the eternal, and the more we walk in the Spirit, the easier it will be to have an eternal mindset.

How to Overcome

Sexual temptation is a powerful weapon for the enemy. If you aren't continually aware of your spiritual condition, wearing divine armor, and marking clear boundaries, then you are vulnerable to the invasion of the enemy.

In the next few paragraphs I've outlined several rules of thumb for you to gauge your sexual boundaries. I want to warn you, these aren't easy. It takes reliance upon the Holy Spirit to see that these boundaries aren't crossed. It's difficult, but there's good news—with God, all things are possible (Matthew 19:26)!

First, if you've never dabbled in sexual activity, don't begin. When I was a little girl, something made me believe that I shouldn't kiss until I was 16 years old. I have no idea if it was the movies or 50's songs that made me think that, but I was determined to hold on to that personal vow. I was actually 18 when I kissed a boy for the first time. It made me nauseous. But for some reason, like a drug, I tried it again (on someone else), and decided that I liked it very much. That was the summer before I left for college. When I got on campus, I was free, unsupervised, and ready to kiss some more. I'm embarrassed now when I think of how many men I kissed.

It was actually much easier to say "no" when I had set the boundary not to kiss *anyone*. It wasn't until my boundary was lifted that sin started to take place in my life. Sin didn't take place right away, but kissing is a slippery slope—getting you more and more involved each time you engage. It was only by God's grace that I was never sexually active. (That was one boundary that wasn't lifted until my honeymoon.) But I did do a lot of things that I now regret.

Dennis and Barbara Rainey, co-founders of FamilyLife, challenged their children to wait until their wedding days to have their first kiss. In their book *Parenting Today's Adolescents*, Dennis tells a story about their son Samuel:

> *[One day] Samuel called from the university he attends. I asked him if I could ask him a gritty question and then if I could use his answer in our book. Always up to the challenge, Samuel said, "Fine, go for it."*
>
> *Going for the jugular I asked, "Have you ever kissed a girl?"*
>
> *Samuel's reply was quick and firm, "Nope! I am waiting until I get to the wedding altar."*
>
> *Probing deeper, I asked, "Have you ever been tempted?"*
>
> *"Sure," he said. "But I try to stay out of situations where that temptation can occur."*
>
> *"When were you tempted?" I went on.*
>
> *I could almost hear him smile over the phone, "Oh, it was before I decided on my standards, in the seventh grade with a girl I liked."*

Samuel did make it to his wedding day, and when he kissed his bride for the first time, it was quite a kiss! But did you notice when the greatest temptation came? *Before he set any boundaries.* Now is the time to decide to remain pure despite the excuses that loneliness brings. Write a letter to yourself or to God, stating your boundaries. Before you go any further down the line of sexual impurity, draw a clear line in the sand.

Second, dress modestly. I am shocked at how I see Christian women dressing today. I realize that the trends are becoming more and more revealing. But I don't remember Jesus commanding us to be trendy. The apostle Paul wrote that it is better not to do anything that will cause your brother to stumble (Romans 14:21).

If Christian women know that their brothers struggle with maintaining pure thoughts, then why don't we do everything we can to dress in a way that avoids temptation? The shorts and skirts are too short and the tops come down too low. I had to stop shopping at one of my favorite stores because I couldn't find anything decent there anymore. I'm not suggesting that we should purposely dress unfashionably, but I am suggesting that we could put a little more effort into finding something that is both fashionable and modest.

As women, we face two problems. One is that we don't understand the power that we posses over men. I was once working as the receptionist in a non-profit organization. I saw the same faces each day as they came in and out of the building, and many of the men worked on the first floor, where the reception desk was located. I always tried to be friendly and outgoing to people, smiling cheerfully as they came and went. One day, an employee named Jack came through the lobby with a friend. As they walked by the desk, I made a friendly comment to Jack (which I can't even remember now.) Before he went around the corner, he stopped, turned around with a sour look on his face and said, "I'll have you know, I am a married man!"

I was stunned. I had no idea what I had said or done to him, but apparently my "friendly" nature looked to him like flirting. I had no idea how powerful a woman's persona can be. I later told a male friend about the incident, and he confirmed that even something as simple as innocent "friendliness" can be interpreted by men as interest.

Now imagine if I had been in the habit of dressing with low-cut tops and short skirts. Jack would have really had a problem on his hands! Who knows if he would have been haunted by images of this young woman at work, dressed provocatively who was just waiting for the day he would show interest in her. Not only would Jack be sinning, but I would be the cause of it!

We women need to have more concern for our brothers' spiritual well being than we have for our fashion. It's more important that our brothers' minds be pure than it is for me to flaunt the latest trends. Even though I was mortified to find out that Jack thought I was attracted to him, I was also proud that he was brave enough to confront me.

The other problem that we women have is a desire to be desired. My mother used to say, "Men struggle with lust, but women struggle with lasciviousness." That is to say that women *want* to be lusted after. It makes us feel powerful, like having a magic spell over men.

I have to admit that it makes me feel great when I see a guy turn his head—it doesn't matter his age, his weight, or his social status. If he takes a double take my way, I smile inside. Why? Because I want to think that like Helen of Troy, someone might launch 1,000 ships for me.

Women who are experiencing loneliness are particularly vulnerable in this area. It's easy to get a lot of attention when you start to wear clothes that reveal parts of your body. But this is not the kind of attention that will lead to a healthy relationship. It is only a temporary superficial fix on a much deeper problem. As someone once said, "It's like putting a band aid on cancer."

The next time you pick out something to wear, notice how you feel. Are you choosing that outfit because you feel like it makes you look sexy? Are you choosing that dress because you know there will be a lot of single men at the event? What if it were a room full of single women? Would you still wear the same dress? Notice your thoughts. Are they on things of God? Would He be honored if you wore that outfit?

There was a time in my early single life when someone challenged the amount of guys that I socialized with. This person told me that it looked like I needed male attention to feel good about myself and questioned whether or not I would ever be able to get married because, "I doubt if you could handle being with just one man."

It was then that I made the decision to stop talking to guys for a season. As I looked around at my friendships, I realized this person was right—almost all of my friends were guys. *Why?* I wondered. *Why don't I connect with girls?* I needed girls in my life for fellowship and pure friendship that wasn't tainted with attraction. For about a year, I did nothing but develop girl friendships. It was very hard to change after all that time, but I learned a lot about myself as a woman and who I was in Christ. What about you? Do you rely on male attention to feel valued? Are you always preoccupied with how to make yourself more attractive so that you can impress men?

Third, limit what your eyes and ears consume. Jesus describes our eyes like windows to the soul (Matthew 6:22-23). If you've ever seen something very disturbing like witnessing a very bad accident, you know how hard it is to get images out of your mind. It's the same with things that we see on the movies or television. The more you see people having sexual relationships outside of marriage, the harder it is to have pure thoughts and the more calloused you'll become to it. Philippians 4:8 says, "Whatever is true, whatever is honorable, whatever is right, whatever is pure, whatever is lovely, whatever is of good repute, if there is any excellence and if anything worthy of praise, dwell on these things." God takes our vision seriously. So seriously, in fact, that Jesus said in Matthew 5:19 that if our eyes offend us, we should pluck them out.

Popular culture tells us it's okay to engage in sexual activities. Look at popular television shows where the characters end up sleeping with each other at different times throughout the season and discuss sex as if it were ice-skating or a walk through the park. They have no respect for the holiness of the sexual act or the fact that it is a serious sin against God when it is performed outside of marriage (1 Corinthians 6:18).

Fred Stoeker, co-author of the best-selling *Every Man* series said,

> *I became a Christian in 1980, about the time many denominations began to relax their standards on Hollywood and the viewing habits of their people. Churches rewrote and watered down their entertainment standards for membership in their by-laws. Eventually, pastors even began using feature films as their message texts.*
>
> *Now, just 25 years later the results are staggering. While mainstream feature films can pollute as surely as pornographic web pages, Christians ignore the truth because everyone else is watching them. These films damage our oneness with Christ as surely as cyberporn.* [13]

Single women are especially vulnerable to romantic comedies. I remember watching those movies, fantasizing that I might one day meet a man like one of the characters in the film. I certainly wasn't thinking about God or spiritual matters.

It's not wrong to watch movies like this, but it is wrong to fantasize about their existence in real life. It's really a kind of soft porn for women. (It's the same with romance novels.) And it's only making you more dissatisfied with where God has you right now facing loneliness. By focusing on what you don't have, you miss out on what you do have—an opportunity to know Christ in a deeper way than ever before. Only He can fulfill you like you want to be fulfilled. Only He can give you the kind of belonging that you hope for. Yet these films and books make you believe that there is a more perfect man out there, and if you can just find Mr. Right all your sorrows will come to an end. It's an outright lie. Don't fall prey to it.

It's funny how after getting married, all of those romantic comedies lost their luster. I know now that marriage is not a cure for loneliness. It's simply a new way to experience Christ.

Another thing that is filling hearts with lies is pornography. This isn't just a problem for men. The Neilsen NetRatings report that one in three visitors to all adult websites are women. They estimate that 9.4 million women in the United States accessed online porn in September 2003. [14]

The porn industry is going gangbusters on the Internet. It's a $57 billion industry worldwide with $12 billion of those dollars generated from the United States alone. [15] The reason? Loneliness.

Patrick J. Carnes is clinical director of Sexual Disorder Services at The Meadows, an internationally recognized, private multiple addiction/disorder treatment and recover facility in Wickenburg, Arizona. He said, "The Internet is not the problem; it is the *solitude and isolation* of the user that can engender the problematic behavior that leads to sexual addiction" (emphasis mine). [16]

You see, when you don't see loneliness through the lenses of the Holy Spirit, you can be tempted to find fulfillment through temporary means. You may be able to live off of "eye candy" for a while, but you will never get the nutrients you need from candy—you must have the Bread of Life, and the two cannot mix. Jesus said, "No one can serve two masters" (Matthew 6:24). Either you will love porn or you will love Christ, but only the latter will fill the void.

Kathy Gallagher is the vice president and co-founder of Pure Life Ministries. In her article "Women and Porn: The Unthinkable Becomes Reality," she tells the story of Julie, a single who fell into the trap of pornography.

> *Before becoming involved in porn, Julie's life would have been considered normal by today's Christian standards. Although she participated in the singles group at her church, she struggled with loneliness. Julie secretly envied the bubbly girls who seemed to attract guys. Sometimes she despaired of ever finding Mr. Right. For some time she had been watching one of the leading networks of soap operas, allowing the immorality portrayed on the show to fuel her secret fantasy of being a beautiful seductress.*
>
> *She was embarrassed one evening when the pastor's wife came for a visit while the show she had recorded that day was playing on her TV. The older woman's face flushed when she saw a torrid love scene. Julie's feigned indignation masked the fact she had come to enjoy this kind of fare. The truth was she continually fostered romantic and sexual fantasies about several male acquaintances at her job.*

Another pastime unexpectedly developed in Julie's life. One day she confided n a girlfriend from church about her struggle with loneliness. Her friend suggested that Julie visit Christian chat rooms on the Internet where she could develop risk-free relationships with men. At first Julie tried it hesitantly and carefully, but before long she was heavily involved. Eventually, she expanded her involvement to include larger, secular chat rooms. Initially, the amount of sexual talk alarmed her, but she gradually became fascinated with it. It made her feel like a star in her own soap opera.

Occasionally, Julie would see messages that linked to adult websites. In the beginning, she resisted her curiosity, but she eventually had no resistance left. One night she impulsively clucked on a link to an adult website. She panicked when an image of a copulating couple popped up on the screen and she quickly closed the site with trembling hands. The scene haunted her memory. A few nights later she revisited the site. She was so enthralled by what she saw that she was completely drawn in. After the exhilaration of that night her soap opera seemed tame and boring. She found herself returning to the adult websites time and again. She knew it was wrong, but, despite repeated promises to quit her behavior, she kept going back to them.[17]

You see, Julie was on a slippery slope. She didn't purposely fall prey to this addiction, but because of her loneliness she let down her guard, looking for a way to cure the pain, and she opened her eyes (and heart) to a life of slavery. The addiction came to rest in her heart, poisoning her relationship with Christ and with other believers.

If you're addicted to porn, this is no small matter. Don't trick yourself into believing that you can "quit anytime." It is an addiction, and it won't be easy to let go of. If you view pornography of any kind, get help as soon as possible, or it will ruin your life.

Not too long ago I ran into an old male acquaintance from my single days. We chatted for a while, and he told me that he and his girlfriend broke up. After seeing him, I couldn't help but try to play a little bit of matchmaking with a close girlfriend. The next time I saw her I said, "Do you remember Rick? I saw him the other night. He is such a nice guy and good looking, too, don't you think? Sounds like he broke up with his girlfriend."

She had already heard about the situation and said, "His girlfriend broke up because he was addicted to porn. Man, I couldn't deal with that."

Rick was a well-respected likeable guy, but now the word has gotten out about his porn addiction. The girls who are trying to find a man who pursues purity are not going to want to date him. Even his girlfriend found it too much to handle.

If you're addicted to porn, it's not too late to find help. In the next section, I will give you several ways to find freedom from this stronghold, including ways to find Christian counselors in your area.

The fourth way to keep your sexual boundaries is to guard your heart. Keep your love for Christ first in everything. The Bible says that the body is the temple of the Holy Spirit (1 Corinthians 10:19). Don't allow unholy things to enter your body; treat it as a sacred place. Have as much respect for your body as you would your church. If you wouldn't listen to a certain kind of music in church, then don't let the lyrics enter your ears. If you wouldn't wear a certain blouse or shorts to church, then don't wear them Monday thru Saturday. If you wouldn't use particular words in church, then don't say them at home.

Also, be picky about the kind of people that you open up to and share your heart with, particularly friends of the opposite sex. Friendships that cross genders almost always lead to deeper feelings for one person or the other. I can't count the number of times I've seen friendships turn unhealthy because girls weren't careful enough about who they shared their heart with. Be selective about the guys that you go out with. Set a high standard of the kind of man you want to marry, and then don't compromise those standards, not even for a "harmless" date.

You not only need to guard things *from* getting into your heart, but you need to *fill* your heart with things that are pure and holy. Memorize scriptures on purity and holy living, and practice their messages. Here are a few you can keep in your heart:

- Do you not know that your body is a temple of the Holy Spirit who is in you, whom you have from God, and that you are not your own? (1 Corinthians 10:9).

125

- Now flee from youthful lusts and pursue righteousness, faith, love and peace, with those who call on the Lord from a pure heart (2 Timothy 2:22).

- Finally, brethren, whatever is true, whatever is honorable, whatever is right, whatever is pure, whatever is lovely, whatever is of good repute, if there is any excellence and if anything worthy of praise, dwell on these things (Philippians 4:8).

Don't take your sexuality lightly. It's like a precious piece of china. When it is used in the correct context, like a dinner party, it is useful and beautiful. But when it is used out of context, like a picnic, it is prone to being chipped and broken. You can never take too many precautions when it comes to preserving your sexuality.

Taking Extreme Measures

Many of you reading this book are living a life of impurity right now, and the issues that we've already discussed will not be enough for you to stop your addiction. You must take extreme measures.

The Bible tells us to flee youthful lusts (2 Timothy 2:22). Notice that it doesn't tell us to "turn our backs" or "just look away," but it tells us to FLEE! It's not enough to try to withstand the temptation; it should be as far away from you as possible.

Many people get married thinking that marriage will satisfy the constant craving for sex. As a matter of fact 80% of married sex addicts thought the same thing. [18] But this isn't the case. The addiction only grows—no *real* person can satisfy the sex addict's hunger. So the answer isn't marriage, but it's a change in actions. You must choose right now to pursue purity. These three steps will help you.

First, confess that you have a problem. People with a sex addiction often use the excuse that they can "quit any time." But they don't quit— they keep participating, and the conscience becomes more and more calloused. Whether you are participating in sexual activity, viewing porn, or finding that you go too far with physical affection, then you have a problem. None of these activities are pure and in the eyes of God, they are sinful and unholy.

It's important to admit this fact to yourself, but it is equally important to confess it to someone else who will keep you accountable to your decision of purity. Doug Boudinot, director of Ascent Resources, pastor, and a mental health practitioner wrote, "The first step in confessing the struggles [you] face is to carefully choose the appropriate person or persons in whom to confide. Choose one or two grace-giving people who are spiritually mature and have endured some serious pain in their lives. Usually those who know brokenness and are willing to minister out of their brokenness are the safest." [19]

Other people not only provide accountability, but they also help you carry the burden. They can weep with you when you weep and rejoice with you when you rejoice (Romans 12:15). Confess to someone who understands you and has experienced a failure of his or her own. You don't need judgment—God is already convicting your heart. You need a friend who will *help* you. Confess to a friend who will give you grace.

Sheri Rose Shepherd gives several other criteria in choosing an accountability partner:

1. Is the person's walk with God strong and consistent?
2. Does this person love you enough to be truthful with you?
3. Can you trust this person to keep your personal matters private?
4. Will this candidate take seriously the job of holding you accountable?
5. Do you feel comfortable being honest and transparent with this person?
6. Will this partner in the faith continually pray for you?
7. Will this person make time to call you or meet with you once a week to keep up with what you are doing? [20]

If you aren't brave enough to confess to someone right now, then practice confessing anonymously. Call a trusted ministry or non-profit organization and talk to an operator about your problem. Write an e-mail or a letter with no name or return address and then send it. By practicing the discipline of confession, you will become more used to the fact that you do have a problem. Although this is a good practice, anonymous confession is not enough. Eventually, you should confess face to face to a friend who can help you. Yes, there is an amount of shame involved in this, but that is exactly the tool God can use to bring healing to your life.

Another good resource is accountability groups. Find a group or start one with other men or women. Make sure you find others that are of your same gender, so that the sexual addiction is not tempted as deeper relationships form with others that are going through this trial with you.

Second, take extreme measures to ensure your safety. Imagine you're driving down a thoroughfare, and you see a person walking or riding a bike near the road. What do you do? In most cases, you would steer far clear of the individual, getting as far away as you can to keep from possibly injuring that person. In reality, there is plenty of room between the vehicle and that person in order for him or her to have safe passage, but drivers practice extreme safety in order to *make sure* there are no accidental collisions.

The same is true for sexual addiction. Sometimes you must go out of your way to make sure there is no temptation. It's a security measure, and it's well worth it. A friend of mine in college felt he was so tempted by sex that he gave up kissing until he was married. He knew that the slippery slope was too steep for him to resist, even with just a simple kiss, so in order to ensure his purity he took extreme measures. By the way, he eventually married a girl who had never been kissed, and they kept their promise till the moment the pastor said, "You may now kiss the bride."

In an interview on "FamilyLife Today," Joshua Harris, author of *Boy Meets Girl* said:

> *Lust comes with a lie. A little sinful fantasizing won't hurt. Lust says taking radical action against sin isn't necessary. We've all heard that line—"Well, you don't have to get radical about this," and yet Romans tells us that setting our mind on the flesh brings death. Galatians says that sowing to the flesh brings spiritual ruin and corruption ...*
>
> *Lust comes with the lie that God won't mind a little compromise, and yet Colossians 3 says put to death whatever belongs to the earthly nature. Because of these, the wrath of God is coming ... God is holy, and His wrath is coming on this very sin.*[21]

I do not believe that everyone must swear off kissing in order to maintain purity. But I would like to challenge you—if you've experienced difficulty in remaining pure, take extreme measures. Do *whatever* it takes to ensure the safety of your purity. For some, that means no dating. For others, no kissing. For others, no television, Internet, or magazines (even if you read them "just for the articles.") Like Harris says, be radical.

Extreme actions like these may earn you some strange looks. Some people may even take *offense* to your radical views. But remember that what God thinks of your life means more than what any man in this world thinks.

Third, seek help from professional services. There are counselors who can help you. There are ministries that specialize in sexual sin and addiction.

There are also a number of software products available that you can download on your computers. Twenty percent of young people who use the Internet regularly are exposed to unwanted sexual approaches. Twenty-five percent encounter unwanted pornography[22]. If these types of precautions had been put in place, the innocence of these kids would have been spared.

No matter how far you must go to find healing from sexual sin, it's worth it. You will never find peace in your heart while living in a life of sin. If you want to experience the blessings of loneliness, God will give you the grace to overcome.

Chapter 11

The Good News

"For God so loved the world that He gave His only son that whoever believes in Him will never die, but have eternal life."
-John 3:16

There was a man dropped by helicopter in the middle of a forest. He was given all the tools he needed to survive and to make it back to his home: a map, a compass, and plenty of food and water tied in a sack with a combination lock. He even had the code to unlock it written on a sheet of paper. He had every tool he needed to survive, but there was one major problem: He was blind.

No matter how many tools this man was given, none of them did him any good because not only could he not see where he was going, he couldn't read the compass or the map and he couldn't see the numbers to open the lock for food or water. What he needed more than anything was sight.

You may be reading this book like that blind man in the forest trying to read a compass. You have no idea what I mean by "Christ living in you." You want what I have described—the love, joy, and peace that comes with the suffering of life. You can see that what Christianity offers is good, and something inside you tells you this is right, but you don't know how to receive it. It makes no sense.

My friend, there is hope for you. Jesus Christ is well known for giving sight to the blind. All it takes for salvation and the abundant life is faith, confession, and repentance.

The Ten Commandments

Every man and woman on the earth is a sinful person—we have all broken God's law in one form or another, and no one is good enough to get to heaven on his own merit. "But," you may be saying, "I *am* a good person. I have never killed anybody or stolen a lot of money."

What you don't understand is that God's standard for heaven is perfection. That means any sin, large or small, is still a sin, and makes you imperfect. Any sin, no matter the size, deserves the penalty of eternal damnation in Hell.

Are you familiar with the Ten Commandments? In Exodus 20, God summoned Moses to Mt. Sinai where He gave Moses His laws for man. This was the standard by which He was to make His judgments for His people. In essence, the commandments are as follows:

1. You shall have no other gods before me.
2. You shall not make yourself any graven image.
3. You shall not take the name of the Lord your God in vain.
4. Remember the Sabbath day to keep it holy.
5. Honor your father and your mother.
6. You shall not kill.
7. You shall not commit adultery.
8. You shall not steal.
9. You shall not lie.
10. You shall not covet (want what others have).

This was the standard that God set in order for a person to get to heaven. As you look at these laws, I hope you realize that you have broken some of them, such as, telling a lie (even a small one), or stealing (even a piece of gum or quarters from your mother's purse). There are also many of these laws that you have broken yet may not even realize it.

For example, Jesus said in Matthew 5:27-28 that if you lust, then you have committed adultery in your heart, and He also said in Matthew 5:21-22 that if you call your brother a fool that you are in danger of Hell fire.

These standards are very high, and to break them is punishable by eternal damnation in Hell.

"Well, everyone sins," you might say, and you're right. Romans 3:10 says, "There is none righteous, no not one." Every one of us is guilty.

Romans 3:23 says, "All have sinned and come short of the glory of God." None of us can live up to that standard, and therefore we deserve Hell.

A Way Provided: A Ransomed Life

Even though God is perfect and demands perfection, He is also gracious and loving. The Bible says that God is not willing that any should perish (2 Peter 3:9). So He provided a ransom for our lives—a man innocent of sin who would take our punishment for us. God sent His only Son to die our place. The name of this man is Jesus Christ. His blood paid the ransom for our souls so that we would not suffer eternal death in Hell. As John 3:16 says, "For God so loved the world, that He gave His only begotten Son, that whosoever believeth in Him should not perish, but have everlasting life" (KJV).

What Jesus did for us was not just a kind act, but it was a miracle. Because Jesus was perfect, innocent, and sinless, death had no power over Him. In three days, Jesus rose from the dead, having conquered sin and death for all eternity (Romans 6:9, Revelation 1:18). Now, as a result, a way has been made for you and me to go to heaven and spend eternity with our Father, having been freed from the bondage of our debt.

In order to enjoy this salvation, here is what you must do—confess the sins that have kept you separated from God and turn away from those things and put your faith and trust in Jesus Christ as Lord and Savior of your life. Once you do this, ask the Spirit of God to come into your heart, and He will give you a new life with new desires, and you must put on the righteousness of Christ. Ray Comfort of Living Waters Ministries describes putting your faith in Christ like putting on a parachute. You don't just look at a parachute and *believe* that it will save you, but you put it on. It is the same with the righteousness of Christ. Do not go on sinning like the hypocrites, but follow the righteousness of Christ. All of this is done in His power and strength, which He gives freely to you.

The Bible says that if you believe in God's Son, Jesus, putting your faith in the sacrifice that He made for you, and if you believe that He has risen from the dead, you will be saved from Hell and adopted into God's family as His child (Acts 16:31).

If this is the desire of your heart, then don't wait any longer to receive Christ as your Savior. Don't go on with the unanswered questions and the heartbreak that so often consumes your life. Come to know the perfect

133

Bridegroom that I talked about earlier. With Christ, you are never alone, even in the midst of loneliness. Jesus said, "I am with you always, even unto the end of the world" (Matthew 28:20 KJV). If you have a Bible, read the Gospel of John. This will go into further detail about the life of Christ and His teachings.

Beginning a New Life

Becoming a Christian is not magic. It doesn't mean that everything will be a bed of roses or that you will never struggle again. As I stated over and over in this book, suffering is part of the Christian life. Jesus said, "If any man will come after me, let him deny himself, and take up his cross, and follow me. For whosoever will save his life shall lose it: and whosoever will lose his life for my sake shall find it" (Matthew 16:24-25). Taking up a cross is painful. But just like I also told you, those times of struggle will help you grow closer in your walk with Christ, and you will not go through suffering without meaning or purpose.

Your next step as a new believer is to *find a church family*. These are our brothers and sisters in Christ who will encourage and help you during times of temptation and help you grow. They are like-minded, providing accountability when you go through trials, and they lift you up in prayer when you need strength. There is power when several believers are together. Jesus said, "Where two or three have gathered together in My name, I am there in their midst" (Matthew 18:20).

The teaching of the pastor will also help you continue to grow in your new faith. And you will have the pleasures of taking part in corporate worship.

Some people mistakenly believe that they can brave the Christian life alone, and choose not to attend church, but Hebrews 10:24-25 says, "And let us consider how to stimulate one another to love and good deeds, not forsaking our own assembling together, as is the habit of some, but encouraging one another…" The Christian walk is not a one-man show. We need the camaraderie of one another in order to fight the battles of our enemy.

In addition, start reading the Bible as it is the Word of God. John 1:1 says, "The Word was God." Everything you read in the Bible is the very heart of God. Read it, study it, and memorize it. With the Bible you are no longer the blind man walking with all of the tools and no way to see them. If you believe in Jesus, then you have been given sight. Follow Jesus, and you will never stray from your path. Prayer is your compass and the Bible is the map to show you the way.

Staying Strong

I want to warn you; we do have an enemy. Be careful of pitfalls and traps along the way. 1 Peter 5:8 admonishes us, "Be of sober spirit, be on the alert. Your adversary, the devil, prowls around like a roaring lion, seeking someone to devour." But the word of God says you can resist him and he will flee from you (James 4:7). Do not be afraid, though, because you are on the winning side. As 1 John 4:4 says, "You are from God, little children, and have overcome them; because greater is He who is in you than he who is in the world." Jesus has already conquered the power of Satan, and Jesus lives in you! The devil will try to deceive you into thinking that he is something to be feared, but don't listen to his manipulation. The power of Christ is greater.

Also, don't be fooled by false teachers. You will only know the difference by testing everything by the word of God. The more you know the scripture, the more equipped you will be. The Bible says that the word of God is a sword (Ephesians 6:17), so learn to use it in the battles.

There are many great resources that can help you begin your spiritual walk. Here are a few of my personal favorite teachers and communicators of the gospel:

The Pleasures of God by John Piper
His Intimate Presence by Bill Bright
Becoming a Woman of Excellence by Cynthia Heald
Singled Out for Him by Nancy Leigh DeMoss

God bless you as you begin this new spiritual journey through life. Don't worry if you trip or fall and sometimes can't seem to find your way. Just call out to Christ, who is the way, the truth, and the life (John 14:6), and He will come to your rescue.

I love the song "I Need a Hero" by Christian recording artist Chris Rice, in which the writer confesses:

135

Well, I don't quite know how to do this
But Jesus, I can't save myself
So here I go calling out for mercy
And crying out for your help

(So if you hear me. . .)
I need a hero
Please dare to find me
Fly to my rescue
And crash through the wall
Announce my freedom
Bring me to my senses
Gather me into your strong arms
And carry me off.[23]

I can't tell you how often I feel this way. I've been a believer in Christ most of my life, and I'm still amazed at how often I fail. I doubt God; I try to do things on my own; I believe the lies of Satan. Yet the Father's mercies are new every morning (Lamentations 3:23). No matter how great my sin, God's grace is greater. Because of His love for me, I love Him more and more each day.

One last thing, don't hide this Good News. Tell others about what Christ has done for you. Tell your friends, family, and even strangers. Bill Bright said that less than two percent of Christians share their faith regularly. Don't be a part of this statistic. This news is just too good to keep it all to ourselves! If you have the cure for cancer, would you not share it?

We all need Jesus to rescue us—we can't save ourselves. So when you feel like life is just too hard, cry out to Him, and He will not forsake you. Depend on Him, not on yourself because none of us have the power to change ourselves—only Christ can do that. You don't have to be perfect because Christ was perfect for you, and now His Holy Spirit lives in you.

Chapter 12

Morning Will Come

"Whoever wishes to save his life will lose it; but whoever loses his life for My sake will find it."
                                        -Matthew 16:25

The warmth of Michael's body was coming through her. Mara felt the weight of his arm across her and the solidness of him bracing her back. She looked at the stars, tiny jewels against black velvet. She had never seen it like this before, so close she felt she could reach up and touch each bright speck of light. The night sky was beautiful. It had never looked like this from a window. And the smell—thick, moist, earthy. Even the sounds around her became a kind of music, like the birds and insects, like the rain plinking into the tin cans of a dingy wharf shack. Then the darkness lightened.

It began slowly, hardly noticeable. The stars grew smaller and smaller, and the black softened. She stood up hugging the quilt around her, watching. At her back was darkness still, but before her was light: pale yellow growing brilliant, gold-streaked with red and orange. She had watched sunrises before from within walls and behind glass, but never like this, with the cool breeze in her face and wilderness in every direction. She had never seen anything so beautiful.

Morning light spilled slowly over the mountains, across the valley to the cabin and the woods behind, and up the hillside. She felt Hosea's strong hands on her shoulders.
"Mara, that's the life I want to give you."
The morning sunlight was so bright it hurt her eyes, blinding her more than the darkness ever had. She felt his lips against her hair. "That's what I'm offering you … I want to fill your life with color and warmth. I want to fill it with light."[24]

That's a passage from the book *Redeeming Love* by Francine Rivers, in which a kind Christian farmer marries an embittered prostitute. Throughout the book, the prostitute, Mara, rebels against the love that is freely given to her. The reader wonders why a woman who has had such a hard life would fight so desperately against a man who loves her so much. But we are given glimpses of this woman's heart, and we see the hurt from her past—how she has learned to harden herself against any hope of love, just so she can survive.

If she would only let go and trust him! But in reality, regarding our relationship with Christ, we are often exactly like poor Mara—distrusting the One who loves us so deeply. We look so often at the reflection of the past, not allowing the hurt to penetrate us and lead us through darkness, desperately fighting to save our lives. But we must enter the darkness so we can see the sunrise He is offering.

Jesus said, "Whoever wishes to save his life will lose it; but whoever loses his life for My sake will find it (Matthew 16:25). Mara lives in spiritual darkness, and Michael offers her a new life. Isn't that exactly what God is saying to us? He wants to bring not only light to our lives, but a sunrise full of color and brilliance, chasing away the darkness with more power than we have ever known.

Right now, you are in a time of bitter dark loneliness but hopefully after reading this book you are beginning to embrace it for all it's worth, seeking the purpose of Christ in this valley. You may feel like Mara, looking at the beauty of the darkness for the first time, instead of fearing it. You can finally hear the chirps of the birds and insects and see the jewels of the stars. But the beauty you find in this darkness is nothing compared to the magnificent sunrise you will experience when it's over.

You may have suffered for a long time, and you're wondering how long this pain will go on. Don't underestimate the power of Christ—the light *will* come! You may feel like you're sitting underneath the dark sky of loneliness, not knowing how long it will endure. But I promise, if you sit there long enough, the sun *will* rise.

During the daylight, the position of the sun tells us the time of day— morning, noon, and sunset. But that is not the case in darkness. The position of the moon and stars tell you nothing of the hour. You would simply have to wait the night out until morning. There's an old saying that says, "It is always darkest before dawn." If you feel like you're facing your darkest hour, don't give up; you could be on the verge of daybreak.

Yes, you will hurt for a time, and maybe even a long time. My suffering of loneliness has come and gone, two different seasons each lasting about three years before the Lord brought me two different wonderful husbands. God will not put us through any temptation that we can't handle (1 Corinthians 10:13). He knows how much we can endure and for how long. You can trust God to sustain you through the darkness of this pain, and when it's over, there will be much rejoicing. As Psalm 30:5 says, "Weeping may endure for a night, but joy comes in the morning."

Engaging the Battle

The Christian life is hard. The Bible tells us that we do not fight against flesh and blood but against powers in the heavenly places (Ephesians 6:12, 2 Corinthians 10:3-4). The spiritual battle is more real than the one soldiers fight on foreign soil—it's a battle that takes place in the heart and soul, something that cannot be seen or touched with human abilities. That's why we're exhorted in Ephesians 6:10-18 to put on the whole armor of God so that we may withstand the schemes of the Devil.

- Gird your loins with truth (vs. 14)
- Put on the breastplate of righteousness (vs. 14)
- Shod your feet with the preparation of the gospel of peace (vs. 15)
- Take up the shield of faith (vs. 16)
- Take up the helmet of salvation (vs. 17)
- And take up the Sword of the Spirit, which is the word of God (vs. 17)

There will be times when you will have to engage in the battles that loneliness brings. You may be tempted to marry someone who is not a born-again believer in Jesus Christ. You may be tempted to blame God for your pain and dishonor Him with your tongue. There may be moments of enticement to lust or have sex outside of marriage. And so we must put on the armor to battle—don't give in!

Resting in Christ

There will also be times when you need to rest. You will eventually grow weary from war and feel weak in the soul, especially as you go through the valley of loneliness and a broken heart. During those times it's difficult to engage in battle. We are called to fight, but we are also called to rest. When emotions overwhelm you, challenging you to give up, then rest. Rest in the shadow of the Father's wings (Psalm 57:1). Take refuge in Him (Psalm 34:22). Rest your head upon His chest (Psalm 131:2).

One of the most famous Psalms of the Bible is Psalm 23. In those times when you need respite, read this passage. You may even want to memorize it.

The Lord is my Shepherd, I shall not want.
He makes me lie down in green pastures; He leads me beside quiet waters.
He restores my soul; He guides me in the paths of righteousness for His name's sake.
Even though I walk through the valley of the shadow of death, I fear no evil, for you are with me; Your rod and Your staff, they comfort me.
You prepare a table before me in the presence of my enemies; you have anointed my head with oil; My cup overflows.
Surely goodness and lovingkindness will follow me all the days of my life, and I will dwell in the house of the Lord forever.

Notice the picture the psalmist paints—lie down in green pastures, lead beside still waters ... not much battling going on. Even when walking through the valley of the shadow of death, the psalmist does not fear because the spirit of God is with him.

141

Sheep are helpless to fight on their own—they have no natural defenses, so the shepherd must fight off evil for them, using the rod and staff as weapons of protection. You may be in that place right now—totally vulnerable without defenses. But like the writer of the Psalm, you need not fear. The shepherd will protect you.

A shepherd's staff doesn't just protect the sheep from predators, but it also disciplines them, keeping the sheep from straying too far away. We can be comforted by the control that the shepherd has over the flock both to protect and to reign.

Experiencing the pain of loneliness is like going through a valley of death, as well—the death of yourself. But as you rest in the pastures, you can be comforted knowing that Jesus is with you. Trust in Him and rest, knowing that everything will turn out as it should. You will make it safely to the other side if you follow the shepherd.

There are times during my married life that I miss the blessings of loneliness. Even though I had two wonderful marriages, knowing that each was a calling in my life and completely of God, still there were times when I missed the unconditional love I found during the darkest part of my life. I missed it not because it is such a wonderful place to be, but because of the way the pain forced me to depend on Christ.

During your times of battling through loneliness, there will be many sorrows, but remember that wherever there is rain, there is a rainbow. Psalm 34:18 says, "The Lord is near to the brokenhearted and saves those who are crushed in spirit." Look for the rainbow that God puts in your life—they are there, even if they were created with your own tears.

No matter how dark your situation may seem, you have not been left alone. You are never alone (Matthew 20:8). The Father will fill you with abundant life, even in the midst of loneliness, if you will seek Him and draw close to Him. James 4:8 promises, "Draw near to God and He will draw near to you." How do you draw near? Read the Word and pray daily. Ask God to reveal to you His will in your life and obey His commands.

Commit today to seeking Christ in the midst of your suffering. Are you willing to follow Him in His death? Are you willing to lay down marriage is that is His plan for you? Are you willing to wait for the right person, no matter how difficult the journey?

Most of us struggle with a desire to "get things right." Instead of seeking God's will, we seek to please men and "keeping up with the

Joneses." We compare our lives with others' and want to be looked at and admired. So people get married to fulfill the expectations of others. Or they date someone too long or give in to sexual temptation to please a boyfriend. Today, lay down your will and allow Jesus to live through you. Seek to please God and follow *His* will, not others: You don't have to be the prettiest, nicest, most prestigious—just let Christ glow from your being.

If you will put your faith in Him, you can let go of the anxiousness in your heart to figure out how to fix your problems. Stop trying to carry the burden of the world on your shoulders and team up with Christ. "For my yoke is easy and my burden is light," Jesus says (Matthew 11:30).

Loneliness is a gift. Don't waste what you have been given by seeking to stop its pain. Embrace it for all its worth. Embrace the healing, the humility, the hope. It is suffering that must take place before we can know God for all that He is and the depth of His heart. You cannot know healing without brokenness. You cannot know light without darkness.

If you take advantage of this time, you will not only find your deepest fulfillments in Christ, but you will be one of the few who has experienced all the blessings of loneliness.

Notes

[1] Gonzalez-Balado, Jose Luis and Playfoot, Janet N., *My Life For the Poor*, (Ballantine Books; Reissue edition, 1987), 111.

[2] Tozer, A.W., *The Root of the Righteous*, (Camp Hill, Pa.: Christian Publications, 1986), 137.

[3] Bright, Bill, *His Intimate Presence: Experiencing the Transforming Power of the Holy Spirit.* (Orlando, Fla.: New Life Publications, 2003), 41.

[4] Piper, John, *Don't Waste Your Life* (Crossway Books, 2004), 71.

[5] DeMoss, Nancy, Brokenness: *The Heart God Revives*, et al., 112

[6] Hurnard, Hannah, *Hinds Feet in High Places.* (Destiny Image Publishers, 2005)

[7] Gonzalez-Balado, Jose Luis and Playfoot, Janet N., *My Life For the Poor*, et all., 40.

[8] Hersh, Sharon A., *Brave Hearts*, (WaterBrook Press, 2000), 75.

[9] Transcript, "FamilyLife Today," (Little Rock, Ark.: FamilyLife, 2001), http://www.familylife.com/fltoday/default.asp?id=2966

[10] "Your Looks: What the Voices Say and the Images Portray," The Journal of Biblical Counseling (1997), vol. 15, no.2, Winter: 39-43. Copies of the journal may be ordered by contacting the Christian Counseling and Educational Foundation, 1803 East Willow Grove Avenue, Glenside, PA 19038.

[11] Simon and Garfunkel. "I Am a Rock." *Sounds of Silence.* Simon, 1966.

[12] Shepherd, Sheri Rose, *My Prince Will Come*, pg. 119.

[13] Stoeker, Fred, *Every Man's Battle*

[14] Collum, Jason, "A Woman's Struggle" AFA Journal (March 2004): 20, 21.

[15] 2004 TopTen Reviews, Inc.

[16] "Old Temptation: New Technology." Enrichment. p.23. Fall 2003.

[17] "Women and Porn: The Unthinkable Becomes Reality."

[18] "Prison of Silence: Guidelines to Free Clergy from Sexual Sin" p. 61

[19] "Prison of Silence: Guidelines to Free Clergy from Sexual Sin" p.61

[20] Shepherd, Sheri Rose, *My Prince Will Come*, pg. 203.

[21] "Finding the Power to Change," "FamilyLife Today," 10/28/2003

[22] "Prison of Silence: Guidelines to Free Clergy from Sexual Sin" p.25

[23] Chris Rice. "I Need a Hero." *Deep Enough to Dream.* Rice, 1997

[24] Rivers, Francine, *Redeeming Love*, pp. 139-140.

Made in the USA
San Bernardino, CA
20 January 2015